Vocal Yoga

The Joy of Breathing, Singing
and Sounding

HEATHER LYLE

BLUECAT MUSIC
& PUBLISHING

First Edition

The ideas, procedures and suggestions contained in this book are not intended as a substitute for consulting with your physician. Neither the author nor the publisher shall be liable or responsible for any loss or damage allegedly arising from any information or suggestion in this book.

Published by Bluecat Music & Publishing
Pacific Palisades, CA 90272
www.vocalyoga.com

ISBN: 978-0-9826150-9-6

Library of Congress Cataloging-In-Publication Data Available

All illustrations are from Henry Gray's *Anatomy of the Human Body* and are used with authorization from Bartleby.com, Inc.

Cover Design: Jason Reim
Book Design: Patricia Bacall
Printed in the United States of America

Om Lokah Samastah Sukhino Bhavantu

Contents

Contents

Contents

Chapter Nine – Tension and the Singer

PART THREE: Discovering Your Vocal Beauty

Chapter Ten – Resonance

CONTENTS

CHAPTER EIGHTEEN – POWER PERFORMANCE TOOLS

CHAPTER NINETEEN – TIPS FOR SONG CHOICE

CHAPTER TWENTY – FINAL THOUGHTS

WHAT IS VOCAL YOGA?

I HAVE BEEN A PROFESSIONAL singer for twenty-five years and a yoga practitioner for thirty-five years. When I completed my university studies in voice and began teaching, I realized that the process of transforming the voice was a "yoga" unto itself. The literal translation of yoga is union; therefore, vocal yoga means vocal union. The state of vocal union is a state that we all universally desire. I believe that everyone can have a beautiful, resonant voice and I have made it my personal quest to assist all in finding the voice that reflects his or her true nature.

This book began as a leaflet of vocal exercises. The leaflet got thicker and thicker as I added more exercises and is now a book. Throughout this book, I have attempted to write down most of the techniques that I use that can help the student free the voice. Some of the techniques I created by exploring the link between yoga and the voice and some of the techniques have been passed down to me in the oral tradition through workshops, voice teacher conferences and private lessons. Many of the exercises are a result of my studies in historical vocal pedagogy at Indiana University under Paul Kiesgen. My first voice mentor Louise Caselotti, one of the teachers of Maria Callas, was the first to introduce me to the link between yoga and the voice. Catherine Fitzmaurice has been the most recent influence on my work and the integration of yoga and voice work.

I have added some anatomy and physiology to the book that I use in my teaching practice. I find that the student who understands how his or her body works has an easier time understanding how to use it. My motivation is to help you, the seeker, to find and free your voice. I hope that there is something in this book that will help you on your vocal journey and that you have fun in the process.

Acknowledgments

I am forever grateful to my amazing husband who always gets roped into some type of involvement in all of my ventures and adventures, whether he wants to or not. Thank you for your sharp eyes and intellect and always being there for me.

Thank you to Catherine Fitzmaurice who transformed my teaching in such a profound way that I will never resemble a normal singing teacher again.

Thank you to Jason Reim, artist extraordinaire, who cheerfully created art to fulfill my every whim and actually created a cover with a mandala and light beams!

Thank you to Terrie Barna for your generosity of spirit and superb proofreading.

Thank you to Margo Stuart for your wonderful proofreading and helpful suggestions.

Thank you to Laura Rift, the comma queen, for your excellent final proofreading; your help was invaluable.

Thank you to Patricia Bacall for your beautiful interior design work and your sage advice and support. Your creativity took my book to the next level.

Introduction

O UR SOUND IS OUR ESSENCE. It is pure, it is perfect, it is unique. As far back as 500 BC, the Greek philosopher Pythagoras was experimenting with sound as a healing tool. According to Pythagoras, "Each celestial body, in fact each and every atom produces a particular sound on account of its movement, its rhythm or vibration. All the sounds and vibrations form a universal harmony in which each element, while having its own function and character, contributes to the whole." We are each an individual sound and, at the same time, a part of a universal harmony. Our sound is capable of great subtlety and power. Softly it can soothe and calm. Fully released, our sound fills our mouth, our throat, and opens into our body, spreading to our extremities. Every capillary and organ in our body can be filled with sound. Sound is not restrained by tubes or tubules; it can vibrate into the core of our cells and float through our cell walls free of restriction.

Many of us have become disconnected from our voices and do not know their unlimited possibilities. All is not lost; we can reconnect to our voice and pure vocal behavior most of us had as small children. With Vocal Yoga voice work we can discover and fall in love with our own authentic voice all over again. Our beautiful, resonant voice has only been sleeping, waiting to be gently nudged awake.

Part One

Preparing the Body

We react to pain, fear and external stimuli in manners very similar to the animal kingdom. We have unconscious survival instincts that are deeply rooted within us. Holding our breath and bracing our muscles serves as a survival mechanism.

Chapter One

WHY WE DON'T BREATHE

CAN YOU REMEMBER WHEN YOU were a little toddler and ran around screaming, singing and making funny sounds? Babies and small children are natural breathers and are vocally uninhibited. However, as school begins and the stresses of life accumulate, their breathing begins to change. Children stop breathing deeply and by the time they are adults, most have become disconnected from their breath.

Human beings are very complex and multilayered creatures. We have two nervous systems: our central nervous system, which allows us to exert conscious control over our body, and our autonomic nervous system, which is responsible for complex body functions such as our digestion and heartbeat. The autonomic nervous system is also responsible for the fight or flight mechanism, which controls body reactions such as shivering when cold or frightened. The autonomic nervous system also controls our breathing when we are not consciously controlling it, which is most of the time. Our autonomic nervous system still has behaviors and reactions similar to any other animal on the planet. In many ways, we are not that different from our simian ancestors. We react to pain, fear and external stimuli in manners similar to the animal kingdom. We have unconscious survival instincts that are deeply rooted within us. Holding or bracing our breath serves as a survival mechanism.

Imagine an antelope standing in the woods that suddenly senses a lion lurking nearby. The antelope will freeze and hold its breath to go unnoticed by the lion. We call this body bracing or armoring. Anyone who has ever sat behind the wheel of a car knows what body bracing feels like. We usually experience it as tension in the muscles of our shoulders and neck as the result of gripping the steering wheel to avoid potential disasters. There can be constant stimuli in our lives, of which we may not be wholly conscious, that our body perceives as threats to our safety. We can also body brace in response to emotional stimuli. Have you ever encountered an unpleasant shopkeeper who directed negative energy toward you? You probably held your breath until you were outside the shop. Do you have a boss whose presence, whenever he or she comes near you, causes the muscles in your body to tighten?

Aside from everyday body bracing, more serious physical and emotional stress can be held in our body for years, resulting in poor breathing habits, muscle tensions, poor body alignment and disease. After a physical injury, nearby muscles will begin to guard the injured area, as any movement is painful. Muscles adjacent to an injury will work in a diminished way to keep the affected part stable. The lack of use of these muscles is necessary for the healing of the body; but without physical therapy and breath, the area can stay out of balance with the rest of the body forever. The imbalance between muscles that guard an injury and normal, working muscles can cause stress and distortion in the body. This stress, aside from muscle imbalance, can also lead to a decrease in breathing. Breath creates movement and vibration and, when injured, vibration or movement is what the physical being tries to avoid.

I have been working recently with a lung cancer survivor who was diagnosed last year with nodules on her vocal cords. When she came to my studio, the first thing that I noticed was that she would not breathe below her throat, as she had had chest surgery. It is very normal not to breathe into the chest after surgery. Not allowing the breath to drop into the body can cause vocal cord stress. Overuse of the vocal cords is always an obvious indicator of someone who is not attaching their voice to the breath. So we started working on breathing and singing exercises that strongly stimulated the lungs. Her body's reaction to the breathing was quite strong. Her color drastically changed from a pale grayish shade to a glowing pink. She got dizzy and lightheaded from the oxygen and had to sit numerous times. Although her illness and surgery were long past, her body was still hanging on to the protective bracing behavior it had implemented right after her surgery.

Strong emotional stress will also cause body bracing. We have strong survival instincts to armor our body from perceived pain, emotional as well as physical. The physical being believes that if we do not breathe, we will not feel. Many people who suffer a strong heart-breaking experience will not breathe into the chest. Our voices can be affected by emotional trauma. We can actually get "choked up" when we are filled with emotion. When my mother died I experienced a knot in my throat that would not go away until I realized that I was holding my emotions in my throat. I had to breathe and sound for several weeks, specifically focusing on removing the tension and armoring in my throat.

Post-traumatic stress sufferers often hold their breath. Any traumatic emotional event will cause us not to breathe. I was teaching a class for teenagers and a student's mother came to observe the class and brought along her one-year-old baby. I asked her if maybe she shouldn't stay, as babies usually start to fuss and cry and it can be a distraction to the class. The woman responded that this was her foster child, who was an abused baby, and that the baby doesn't cry or make any sound. I looked at the baby, who was clinging to the woman. As well as not making any sound, the baby was holding her breath. Amazingly, throughout the hour and a half class, the baby did not make a peep.

The body can experience and react to an emotional trauma as extremely as it can to an actual physical trauma. Many people, while suffering a panic attack, feel that they can't breathe and have to be rushed to the hospital in order to be examined for a more serious disorder. They are usually very surprised to discover that their shortness of breath was panic induced.

So, shallow breathing and breath holding are survival mechanisms. Often when students realize that they haven't been breathing, they will say to me with a sheepish look that they are bad breathers. I always tell them not to judge themselves harshly for behavior that was created to protect their physical being. I always say, "Don't get mad at your monkey (what I call the autonomic nervous system) for not breathing; it is trying to help you. Instead, give it a little thank you and show your monkey another way of survival that includes breathing and non-bracing."

Bracing Exercise

Try to watch your breath when you are driving or dealing with a difficult person. Notice if any tension creeps into your body or if you are holding your breath. See if you can breathe and release tense muscles in the moment of a difficult situation.

I always start my classes with the following exercise. Find a partner and put the partner across the room from you. Pick a spot in the middle of the room that you will use as an impact zone. Run toward each other in the direction of the impact zone and barely miss each other. Watch what happens to your body and your breath when you almost collide. Now run toward each other and make a sound at the moment you almost hit each other. Notice what happens to your voice. Some people find that releasing a sound feels good. Many people find that they emit a squeezed, stressed tone. Now run toward each other and at the point of near impact, freeze. Notice any tension in your body, take a breath and exhale with a sigh, relaxing tensed muscles, and then continue on your way. At the point of impact the body will brace to protect you. By becoming aware of the natural instinct of the body to brace under stress, you can eliminate the stress your body perceives by consciously breathing and releasing after an incident of body bracing and "breath holding."

FITZMAURICE VOICEWORK

I am a certified associate teacher of Fitzmaurice Voicework. All of the information in this book pertaining to the autonomic nervous system I learned during my certification. Fitzmaurice Voicework, created by Catherine Fitzmaurice, is one of the leading voice works for actors today. I highly recommend it for actors and anyone who would like to keep his or her body from imprinting stress and creating patterns that may result in disease.

Turning your attention within will make you aware of tight places in your body that you may have had little awareness of before.

Chapter Two

Body Warm-up

A BODY WARM-UP IS STRONGLY advised for singers and actors before singing or acting. In singing and acting, our body is our instrument; so the first thing we want to do is check in with our body. Mentally, scan your body from head to toe and notice any places where there is tension. Because voice work requires us to turn our attention inside our body and feel subtle nuances, most people find that when they start to use their voice, they become aware of tight places in their body that they had little awareness of before.

HIP CIRCLES

Bend your knees and move your hips around in a circle as if you had an invisible hula hoop around your waist that you are trying to spin. Move your hips in a circle to the left and then in a circle to the right, to loosen up the lower back. Make sure to get into the hip joints as well. We spend a lot of time sitting and the hip joints can get very tight. In voice work, we use the spine as a support for the voice. Any tension in the lower spine can affect  the other end of the spine, the neck. Any tension in the neck will negatively affect the voice.

TAI CHI UPPER BODY CIRCLES

Without moving your hips, make circles with the upper part of your body. Bend forward from the upper back, dropping the head forward. Roll the upper body around to the side, then the back, then the other side and back around to the front. A Tai Chi version of this exercise requires you to put your hands on your kidneys while you roll your body around. In the Tai Chi version, your hips can move as well.

STANDING SNAKE

Start by standing. Bend your knees. Imagine there is an invisible ball that you could roll up the front of your body from your shins all the way up to your head. Undulate the whole front of the body as if you were a snake. When lying on the belly, a student doing this exercise looks like a snake or an inchworm inching forward. This exercise stretches the spine from front to back and is fantastic if you suffer from lower back pain due to a tight lower spine.

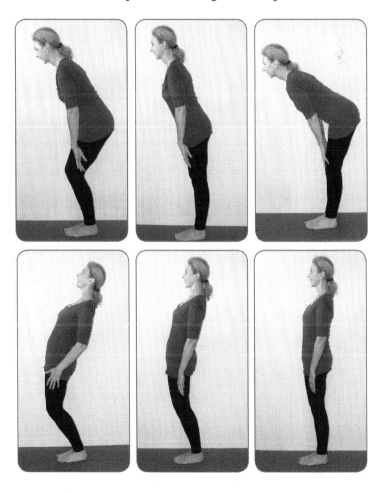

SIDEWAYS SNAKE

While standing, weave your body from side to side like a snake weaving through grass. This loosens up the sides of the body and moves the spine in a sideways manner.

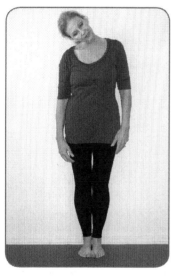

HEAD CIRCLES

Tai Chi masters recommend that we do this exercise daily for energy circulation and tension release. Keeping the neck relaxed, slowly roll your head forward and let the weight of the head fall toward your chest. Gently and slowly, roll the head to the side, to the back and around to the other side. Some people with certain cervical spine problems should not roll their heads to the back. If it doesn't feel good to roll your head to the back, you can just roll your head from side to side.

HEAD SIDEWAYS EIGHTS

A singer wants to have a relaxed head at all times while singing, but one of the major places of tension that voice teachers find in singers is the base of the skull at the back of the head. If the head is not free and floating easily on the cervical spine, the voice will not float easily into the high registers.

Exercise

With the tip of your nose, draw the number eight lying on its side. Then reverse the direction that you draw the figure eight. This exercise relaxes the smaller muscles at the base of the skull and along the cervical spine. This exercise is fantastic to do while singing, especially when trying to reach high notes.

HUGS

Give yourself a big hug. Let your head drop forward and relax. Now hug yourself with the other arm on top. You may notice that this arm and shoulder girdle are tighter than the other side. We always unconsciously choose the more flexible side to stretch first.

ARM SWINGS

Lean a little to the side and let one arm hang from the socket. Swing this arm back and forth as if you were imitating a monkey. Every few swings, let the arm swing completely forward and around, making a circle. Try swinging the arm in the other direction, backwards, around and forward. It is fun to say "weeee" while you do this. Notice if you are breathing or holding your breath while swinging your arm. This exercise is a fun way to loosen up the shoulder girdle.

SHOULDER STRETCH

For singing or speech, we want to keep the neck and shoulders as relaxed as possible. This is the place where most of us hold tension, so this yoga pose is great for relaxing these areas.

Start on the floor on your hands and knees. Move your hips backward until your arms are stretched forward. Take the right arm and slide it horizontally under your outstretched arm with the palm facing upward so that your arms make a "T." Bring your face to the ground and rest the right side of your face on the floor. Rest your forehead on the ground instead if turning the head is uncomfortable for your neck. Feel your shoulder blade sliding down the back of your body as it releases, and keep the top arm extending away from the body as you breathe. Press your left hand into the floor to come back up. Do the other side.

SHOULDER STRETCH WITH STRAP

Take a strap, an exercise band or a long scarf and hold it in front of your body in both hands. Make sure your hands are three feet apart. Still holding on to the strap, inhale and lift your arms over your head and bring them down behind you. Exhale. With the arms still behind you holding on to the strap, inhale and bring your arms back up and over until your arms are in front of you. Exhale. As your shoulders loosen up, you can bring your hands closer together on the strap, but always start first with the hands far apart so that you don't pull any muscles in your shoulders. Start with the exercise being too easy. It is best to be nurturing to the shoulder area. You can make the exercise more difficult when the body is ready.

Body alignment directly affects breathing.
If a person stands with a collapsed chest, he or she
will not be able to breathe from the core of the body
and will not be able to engage the abdominal support
for the voice.

Chapter Three

BODY ALIGNMENT

THE FIRST IMPORTANT ELEMENT IN singing and speech is body alignment. Body alignment is the first thing that voice teachers examine to diagnose breathing problems. Body alignment directly affects breathing. If a student stands with a collapsed chest or has some sort of poor body alignment issue, he or she will find it very difficult to breathe from the core of the body.

Stand and assume a posture that is slumped, depressing the top of the ribcage. Try to breathe from the base of your ribcage. You will find that it will be difficult to breathe below the collarbone, as the top of your lungs are depressed due to your slumped chest. Lift your arms up and over your head and breathe. Notice how, with your arms in the air, it is easy to breathe at the base of the ribcage. Some people even have a sensation of being able to breathe underneath their ribcage. Lower the arms to the side without completely lowering the sternum (breastbone) and ribcage and see if you can still keep the sensation of your breath at the base of, or below, the ribcage.

Feel wide and open across the chest without over-exaggerating the posture, as in thrusting the ribcage forward. Also, do not collapse the chest inward at any time, as is common in slumped posture. Inhale and exhale easily and silently without changing the open posture of ribcage with the sternum elevated.

There is a direct correlation between the position of the sternum and the sides of the ribcage. Put one hand on the side of your ribcage and one hand on your sternum. Breathe, allowing the sternum to rise.

Notice how, when the sternum rises, the ribcage opens. By keeping the sternum lifted, the ribcage stays expanded.

CORRECT POSTURE EXERCISES

One way to check if your body is in alignment is to look sideways into a mirror. There are specific points in the body that we want to line up. If you could draw a straight line down the side of your body, you would want your ear to line up with the tip of your shoulder, which lines up with the top of your hip, which lines up with the side of the knee and the ankle bone. One of the most common out-of-alignment parts of the body is the head. Many people drop their head downward and forward. If the head protrudes forward, the larynx will most likely be in an unfavorable position for phonation.

Find Center Spine

Some people lean backwards when they stand, and some lean forward or to one side. For optimum body alignment and good breathing, the student needs to find the place where his or her spine is perfectly centered between the four directions: north, south, west and east.

While standing, with both feet completely on the ground, lean forward as far as you can without tipping over. Lean backwards as far as you can. Now find a place between the two extremes, in the center, which feels balanced and grounded.

Still standing, lean way to the left and lean way to the right. Once again, find a place that feels balanced in the middle. You have now found your centered spine.

It can be very helpful to have a friend assist you with this exercise. Many students lean backwards without realizing it. A friend can act as a second pair of eyes and give you feedback to let you know if what you think is centered spine really is.

Top to Bottom Centering

Our waist is a movable part. It enables us to bend forward or lean backwards. Above the waist we have our ribcage. Below the waist we have our pelvis. We have already discussed how we want a lifted ribcage floating out of the waist, but we also want a ribcage that is balanced over our pelvis. Without moving your pelvis, stick your chest forward. Now move your chest backwards while stretching your back. Find a place from front to back where your top half feels centered over your bottom half.

Move your hips to the left, move your hips to the right, stick your butt out toward the back and pull your butt forward, tucking your pelvis under. The pelvis is a very movable structure; because of this, many people walk around all day with their pelvis out of alignment.

One of the most common misalignment postures, which we see in singers and actors, is someone who stands sticking his or her butt out. This posture can result in what is called a sway back. The problem with standing with your butt out is that it can cause lower back pain and affect good breathing.

Some singing teachers teach students to always tuck their pelvises under. A slight tucking of the pelvis can be beneficial; however, a too-forward pelvis can be just as harmful for good alignment as a butt-sticking-out pelvic posture. Tuck your pelvis way under and try to breathe freely from the base of the ribcage. What you will most likely notice is that there is tension in the lower half of your body. A mirror is most useful for this adjustment. If your pelvis is out of alignment, when you look sideways in a mirror, the top of your hip joint may not be in line with the side of your kneecap.

STATE OF READINESS POSTURE

Now that you have found center spine, lean back into your heels and try to breathe. You will notice that your breath does not drop into your core easily. Famous voice coach Patsy Rodenburg says that Americans love to stand with their weight in their heels and their pelvises thrust forward. Rodenburg recommends that you shift your weight forward towards the balls of your feet and put your body in an alert state of readiness as if you were going to take a step forward. Take a breath. You will notice that your breath drops into your core easily. Speaking and singing are active actions; both require a state of readiness in the body. Most people have become disconnected from the physicality of voice use and speak or sing in a devitalized way to poor results. The most common standing posture today is one of leaning the weight of the body into the heels. A standing posture of leaning into the heels will often thrust the pelvis forward and will not put the body into an active state. It is a posture of weakness and will not produce a strong voice.

Voice researcher William Vennard (1909-1971), in his 1967 book *Singing: The Mechanism and the Technic*, recommends that the singer stand in an aggressive stance with one foot a little in front of the other. He states, "Above all don't put your weight on your heels. Stand well supported, perhaps a little forward. If your legs weary after considerable singing it is a good thing" (1967, 19).

Exercise for Daily Practice

Whenever you are ready to speak, put your body in a state of readiness with your weight in a slightly forward position on the balls of the feet. Breathe into your core and then speak. Try the same stance for singing.

MOUNTAIN POSE

A wonderful standing yoga pose for body alignment is Mountain. Stand upright with your arms to your sides. Imagine there is a string attached to the top of your head that goes down through the center of your head and attaches to your spine. Remain relaxed and imagine that your head and spine are hanging from this string that is connected to the cosmos. Can you get any taller by stretching your spine upwards? At all times the force of gravity is pressing down on our bodies. Due to the pressure of this gravitational force, our body and spine can start to collapse toward the floor when we are fatigued. "Mountain" can elongate the spine and undo some of the stresses of gravitational force. Also, as we get older, we tend to collapse the space between the base of our ribcage and the top of our hips, as our abdominal muscles that help in structural support get weaker. Do "Mountain" again and pay specific attention to this space and see if you can keep the ribcage lifted from the front and sides of the torso.

RIBCAGE LIFT

When I tell students to lift their ribcages, they will predominantly use their back muscles to do so. Belly dancers and hip-hop dancers learn to lift their breastbone and front of the ribcage by using the front abdominal muscles. See if you can lift your breastbone up and back to normal by only using your abdominal muscles. The space between the top of the hips and the base of the ribcage will increase. Many voice teachers recommend keeping the abdominal muscles toned, as they are important muscles for keeping the ribcage in good alignment, which is paramount for good singing and speaking.

FEET SPINE PREPARATION EXERCISE

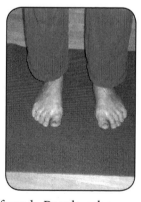

This is a quick but very effective preparation for sounding exercise. It is also great for people with performance anxiety, as it gives your mind something to do in those seconds before singing, acting, or public speaking, when the mind tends to get anxious. Do not skip this exercise. Although simple, this exercise is very profound. People who are connected to their spine are more centered, focused and grounded. Being aware of one's spine also calms the autonomic nervous system. The fight or flight mechanism of the autonomic nervous system can get very active in speaking or singing in public. Feel your feet with your mind. Feel your feet solidly on the ground about a foot apart with your weight evenly on each leg. Find your spine with your mind. The spine also supports the voice, but many of us have little awareness of it. You might want to wiggle a little to feel where your spine is. Feel the lower part of your spine, the middle of your spine and the top of the spine that is your neck. Now that you are in touch with your spine, find the base of your ribcage with your mind, relax your belly and then take a breath, feeling the lower part of the ribcage and your waist expanding 360 degrees around. Take a few breaths and you are ready for performing.

SPINE WALKING EXERCISE

Find your spine with your mind and walk around the room led by your spine. What does that feel like? Your spine has a front, a back and two sides. Do you walk differently? Is your weight balanced differently in your body? Is it pleasurable? F. Matthias Alexander, the creator of Alexander Technique, discovered that most of us tend to move through life led by our chins. Try walking around the room, letting your chin initiate the forward movement of your body. What does this feel like? Alexander recommended that we learn to walk letting the spine lead us instead of the chin.

Since the voice can only go where the breath is, learning to breathe for singing and speech is of the utmost importance.

Chapter Four

BREATHING

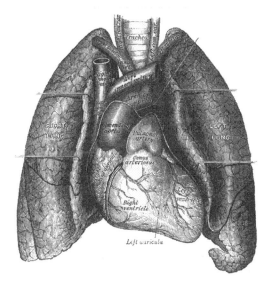

BREATHE=INHALE=INSPIRE=INSPIRATION

Chi sa respirare sa cantare!
One who breathes well, sings well!

THE HISTORIC ITALIAN SCHOOL OF Singing has an old adage: "One who breathes well, sings well." It can also be said that one who breathes well, speaks well. The voice is meant to float out on a stream of air, but most people struggle with this concept. Firstly, many people don't know how to breathe deeply and efficiently, and secondly, they don't know how to excite a stream of air for the voice to spin out on. The result is that most people will breathe shallowly or hold their breath and try to muscle their voice out of their body to poor results. The voice can only go where the breath is, so without breath, we have no voice.

Most breathing is a passive experience unconsciously controlled by our autonomic nervous system, but for singing or mindful speech, we want to use a more active type of breathing. We must learn to intentionally breathe in preparation for voice use. The tendency for new singers or actors, when embarking on voice use beyond everyday speech, is to try to begin sound in the throat. Because we know that our vocal cords are in the throat, many people find it logical to start sound there. In actuality, sound begins with breath. If you just landed from another planet and I told you that your vocal cords were in the core of your body, you would probably use your voice in a healthier way. The vocal cords are only to be used as an oscillator, excited into vibration by the breath coming from below. I have a little mantra I make all my students memorize: *"Breathe first."* Let's learn more about breathing.

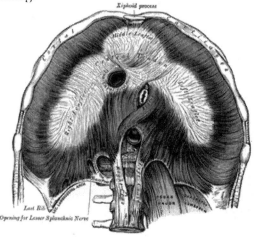

The action of inhalation predominantly uses two major muscle systems, the diaphragm and the muscles of the ribcage called the costal muscles. The diaphragm is a smooth, concave muscle that sits like a dome in the center of the body. It is said to resemble an upside-down bowl. It completely separates the respiratory cavity from the abdominal cavity. In the front of the body it is attached to the base of the sternum (breastbone) and continues its attachment to the lower borders and inner surfaces of ribs seven through twelve, all the way around the back to the lumbar spine.

Inhalation starts with a thought. The brain sends a signal to the cervical spine to activate the nerve from the third to fifth cervical vertebrae to instruct the diaphragm to descend. Simultaneously, the thoracic muscles contract and all three dimensions of the ribcage swing open. Since the pleural membranes of the lungs are attached to the ribs, the lungs are expanded. Due to the expansion of the lungs and descent of the diaphragm, a negative pressure is created in the lungs and the body has the impulse to take in air. Once a balance of air pressure is achieved, the muscles of exhalation take over and the body's impulse is to expel air. The ribcage closes and the diaphragm returns to its initial domed position. We cannot consciously control the diaphragm, but we can affect its action by controlling the ribcage and abdominal muscles that compress the abdominal viscera, exerting an upward force against the diaphragm. Flexibility and an awareness of the ribcage as a separate entity to the torso are most advantageous to the singer or theatrical speaker.

Since the voice can only go where the breath is, learning to breathe for singing and speech is of the utmost importance. Most of us practice what we call clavicular breathing. This means that we only breathe at about the depth of the clavicle (collarbone) of the body. Since our lungs are always filled with air, we can get by in our everyday life with just topping off the lungs with air, but this type of breathing is not sufficient for singing or extended voice use. Clavicular breathing results in a shallow sounding voice that does not resonate within the body. The singer will also have the natural tendency to use the throat as the power center, as his or her awareness and breath have not dropped into the core of the body where the power source of the voice is. Another effect of shallow breathing, which we often see in pop singers, is the use of nasality to make the voice louder. A singer who is unable to use the core of his or her body for strength and support may resort to producing a brassy twang in the nose to create a loud tone.

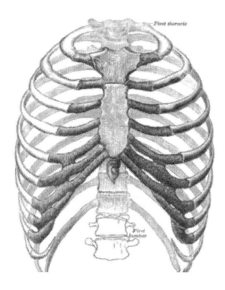

DELAYING EXHALATION

Singing and extended speech are, in fact, delaying exhalation. Conscious inhalation is an active process. The singer or speaker instructs the body to take in air. Exhalation is a passive process in which the muscles of expiration recoil to their pre-inhalation position. For singing or extended speech we want to gain control of the muscles of exhalation to slow down the process of recoil. One way to do this is to have control over the muscles of the ribcage. After the ribcage opens, on inhalation, we want to delay its descent, thus prolonging the position of inspiration and not allowing the exhalation muscles to take over.

The muscles of inspiration are the lowering action of the diaphragm, which causes the abdomen to move outward, and a set of costal muscles that open the ribcage. The exhalation process consists of another set of costal muscles that close the ribcage and the action of the diaphragm as it ascends upward, aided by the abdominal muscles to release any excess air from the lungs. When the exhalation process has completely taken over, we are out of breath and can no longer sing until we take in more air. In singing we learn to pace our exhalation of air more slowly so that we can sing on this air for a longer duration than is necessary for everyday speech. How do we actually do this? We do it by remaining in the position of inspiration as long as we can and delaying the exhalation muscles from taking over. What does this actually mean? The ribcage has a very strong biological impulse, called torque, which propels it to recoil to a closed position after inhalation. The ribcage needs to close to stimulate the body to take another breath. In singing, we want to gain control of torque, to get the base of the ribcage to remain open, so that it doesn't drop until the completion of a phrase. Torque is a very strong biological reflex that takes time to learn to control. At first, when you start training the ribcage to remain open, thus delaying exhalation, the body may resist re-education; therefore, it is very important for the beginning singer to practice breathing exercises often. I have included numerous exercises for this. The Tetrazzini and the Farinelli exercises are two of the best.

The costal muscles and the diaphragm are also very important muscles for health and longevity. They have been called, at times, "the fountain of youth." According to "The National Institute of Aging," pulmonary function measurement is an indicator of general health and vigor and can be used as a primary measurement of potential life span. Singing has been proven to stimulate and improve pulmonary function along with other parts of our body. As we get older, our costal muscles can start to calcify, affecting the radius of expansion of our ribcage. If our ribcage cannot expand, then our lungs cannot completely open and may lose their elasticity. Singing keeps our ribcage flexible and the diaphragm strong. It is not unusual to see singing teachers teaching and singing into their eighties. There are also less obvious parts of our body that are stimulated by singing. Along with the lungs, the heart also sits on top of the diaphragm and is massaged by the more active movements of the diaphragm while singing. The descent of the diaphragm also presses against the contents of the abdomen, massaging the liver and the small and large intestines, stimulating blood flow. So, aside from being fun, singing is good for your health!

AWARENESS OF THE BREATH

To learn to breathe for singing or theatrical speech, we need to increase our awareness of physiological behaviors within the body that we are not normally aware of. How well you can master these new behaviors is influenced by how well you can turn your attention to the inside of your body and become aware of very subtle sensations. Some of the following exercises are purely for awareness and others are to train the body for voice work.

> *Flexibility in the costal muscles of the ribcage is important for good respiratory health. If the ribcage can expand, then the lungs that are housed in the ribcage can fully expand.*

PRANAYAMA BREATHING EXERCISES

Why do breathing exercises? Without breath there is no voice. Singing, chanting or extended speaking is a matter of learning to control the breath. In India, the yogic traditions of breathing exercises and meditations are called pranayama and date to before 300 BC. The Indian sages have long known the power of breath control and have handed down breathing exercises through the centuries. The first known written mention of the breath control techniques of yoga is in *The Yoga Sutras of Patanjali*, written by the great sage Patanjali, somewhere between 300 and 200 BC. Pranayama breathing techniques are now used in yoga studios across the United States and are some of the best exercises to prepare the body for sounding. After studying some of the yoga pranayama techniques, you may wonder if many of the traditional singing exercises were taken from yoga. If you practice these exercises, your breath control will increase and you will become more aware of the sensations and mechanics associated with breathing.

Prana, although used to mean breath, also means all the energy that fills the universe. Yama means control, so pranayama is the control of the breath and life force. When we inhale we are breathing in oxygen, but we are also breathing in cosmic energy. By focusing on the aspect of breath that is universal energy, we can increase our vitality. The yoga practitioner can direct this prana energy to all the parts of his or her body, enriching and invigorating it. Not only does pranayama breathing clean the blood, but it also recharges the life force of the body.

In pranayama, the breathing cycle has been broken down into four parts. Inhalation is called *puraka,* and it is the intake of the life force. Inhalation is an active state; the yogi decides to fill his body with cosmic energy in the form of breath. Exhalation is called *rechaka*. It is passive; the yogi surrenders the breath to be rejoined with the energy of all that is. After inhalation there is a pause before exhalation called *antara kumbhaka,* and after exhalation there is a pause before inhalation called *bahya kumbhaka*. One breathing cycle consists of inhalation, pause, exhalation and pause.

To focus the mind and draw the attention within, away from the senses and exterior world, the yoga practitioner practices increasing the pause of *antara kumbhaka* and *bahya kumbhaka. Kumbhaka* comes from the word *kumbha*, which means a pot that is either empty or full. The torso of the practitioner becomes like a pot that is either full or empty of air. Later we will explore *bandhas*, which are locks that are performed while retaining the breath.

In the following pranayama exercises, breathe through the nose and keep your eyes closed. Do not practice these exercises right after eating. Relax the throat and rest the tongue in the bottom shelf of the mouth and try to remain calm throughout the exercises.

Do not raise the shoulders while inhaling. At first there will be a tendency to raise the shoulders on inhalation, as most of us are used to breathing shallowly instead of from the bottom of the lungs. If you do, the air will not fill the lungs properly and tension will creep into the neck. So focus on filling the lungs with air from the bottom up when you inhale.

Seated Pranayama Exercise

Sit in a cross-legged position or the lotus posture on the floor and close your eyes. Touch your forefinger to your thumb in a circular gesture and rest each hand on each knee. Keep each shoulder down and away from your ears. Relax the muscles of the face and neck, and keep the tongue sitting passively in the bottom shelf of the mouth. Focus the closed eyes gently toward the third eye between the eyebrows. If you cannot sit for long periods on the floor then sit in a chair with both feet flat on the floor. You can also sit next to a wall. Make sure that your sacrum and shoulder blades are touching the wall. Also, make sure that your weight is evenly distributed on each buttock. If you cannot sit with a straight spine, sit on a meditation pillow or a pillow of the same height.

After studying some of the yoga pranayama techniques, you may wonder if many of the traditional singing exercises were taken from yoga.

Begin inhalation from the sides of the waist just below the floating ribs. Fill the ribs from the bottom of the ribcage up to the collarbone. Lengthen the spine vertically as you simultaneously lift your breastbone upward and expand your whole ribcage 360 degrees with breath. There will be a gradual vertical, horizontal and circumferential expansion of the ribcage and the lungs. Keep the abdominal muscles relaxed, and as the lungs fill with air, lift the ribcage up out of the hips, which may cause a narrowing in the waist. Keep a stretch in the front abdominal wall from the pubic bone to the base of the breastbone without tensing the abdominal muscles. Start slowly and only take in as much air as you can calmly control.

Exhalation is normally a passive recoil reflex, but in pranayama we make it an active experience by slowing down and controlling the outflow of the breath stream. B.K.S. Iyengar says that it is of the utmost importance to retain a grip in the costal muscles of the ribcage and floating ribs to control exhalation (2001, 13). Voice teachers are always trying to get students to activate the muscles of the ribcage to control the voice, so this exercise is excellent for singers or actors.

Begin exhalation from the top of the lungs at the point of the collarbone. Exhale very slowly without collapsing the ribcage. Do not collapse the chest, spine or lose the stretch in the abdominal wall from the pubic bone to the breastbone. The ribcage will just slowly decrease in circumference. Feel for the gripping in the costal muscles as the ribcage fights to slow down recoil. Also, go slowly during this part of the exercise. If the air pressure in the lungs becomes uncomfortable or you feel pressure in the temples of your head or you become lightheaded, release the rest of your air and the posture and relax. Pranayama exercises can be vigorous, so gradually build up your endurance. Consult a doctor if you have any cardiac or respiratory problems before practicing pranayama.

Nose Sensation Breathing

Lie down on your back and close your eyes. Put a pillow or a folded Mexican blanket under your head and a pillow or rolled Mexican blanket under your knees.

Exhale to begin. Inhale through your nose and feel the sensation of the air against your nasal passages. When we inhale, the air touches the inner surface of the bottom of the nose. It rides in like a rushing stream down the nasal channel; there is an active sensation to it. Exhale through your nose and feel the different sensation of the air against your nasal passages. When we exhale, the air touches the outer surface of the top of the nose. It floats up and out of the nose channel with a softer, lighter feeling, a more passive sensation. Continue to inhale and exhale for five minutes, while focusing on the sensation of the air entering and exiting the nose. This is a very simple but profound exercise. How many people are aware of the sensation of breath in their nasal passages?

Lung Sensation Breathing

Remove any pillow or blanket from under your head and knees and lie flat on your back. Make sure you are warm and close your eyes. You can also put a piece of cloth over your eyes.

Begin by gently and slowly exhaling (through your nose) all of the stale air from your lungs until they feel empty. Now inhale slowly from the bottom of the lungs, filling each lung up at the same time. Notice that the ribcage expands upwards and outwards as you take in more air. Try your best to coordinate the breath so that each lung fills with air at the same time. Notice if one lung wants to fill faster than the other. Don't judge yourself; just add more air to the emptier lung and keep practicing. Exhale quietly through your nose while trying to evenly expel the air from each lung. Once again, don't judge yourself if your coordination is not perfect. Just keep practicing. Notice how quiet your mind is when you are only concentrating on breathing. This exercise removes any hardness or congestion in the lung tissue. Practice for ten minutes.

Counted Breaths Exercise

The goal of this exercise is to extend inhalation for a period of time and exhale for the same amount of time. Either seated or lying down, close your eyes and exhale to begin the pranayama exercise. Inhale through the nose, filling the lungs from the bottom and expanding the ribcage as in the previous exercise. Inhale slowly to a count of five and exhale slowly to a count of five. Inhale to a count of six and exhale to a count of six. Keep the ribcage active so that you can control the exhalation. Gradually increase the count, only going as far as is comfortable.

Fixed Diaphragm Exercise

Sit in a cross-legged position or the lotus posture on the floor and close your eyes. Gently tense your abdomen so that it does not expand with air. Inhale through the nose and fill the lungs with air from the bottom, expanding the ribcage all the way up to the collarbone. According to yoga traditions, by tensing the abdominal area, the diaphragm is fixed on inhalation. For many people, only the belly fills during inhalation. During this exercise, the ribcage will fill and expand first instead of the belly. This exercise is excellent to prepare the ribcage for singing, although for sound production the abdominals would not be tensed. Later in the book, we will learn about the importance of being able to expand and engage the ribcage for phonation.

A more advanced practice of this exercise is to drop the chin to the chest and rest it on the breastbone, in a chin-lock called *jalandhara bandha,* which is described in the next exercise.

Jalandhara Bandha Exercise

This is a much more advanced pranayama exercise called *jalandhara bandha*. It is another excellent exercise to prepare the body for singing or chanting. Do not try this exercise until you have mastered the previous pranayama exercises.

In yoga, *bandhas* are postures that the practitioner does while doing pranayama. *Bandha* means lock or seal. *Bandhas* help to preserve prana within the body and awaken the *kundalini* energy to rise up the spine. Sit in a cross-legged position or the lotus posture on the floor and close your eyes. Lift the chest and sternum and drop the head into the chin-lock position of *jalandhara bandha*. Bring the head down evenly and rest the chin in the notch between the collarbones. If you have a tight neck, you can roll up a piece of cloth and stick it under the chin. Also, lift the chest up to meet the chin instead of pressing the chin down to the chest. Keep the eyes and nose pointed down towards the chest. Do not collapse the chest. Relax the head and temples. Inhale through the nose. Keep the torso active and hold your breath for four seconds. The torso muscles will be active, but try to relax any unnecessary muscle gripping. Breathe out slowly, controlling the closure of the ribcage. Start very gradually with this exercise. Practice until you can hold the breath for ten or fifteen seconds. If you feel any pressure in the temples or the head, you are exceeding your capacity for breath retention and you must immediately reduce the number of counts for which the breath is held. This exercise gradually introduces your body to an increased amount of oxygen and life force. It is not suitable for those with high blood pressure or cardiac disorders.

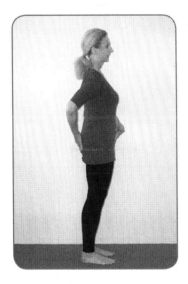

Mula Bandha

In yoga, *mula* means a root and *bandha* means lock or binding. *Mula* refers to the space between the genitals and the anus called the perineum, the actual root of the torso. The perineum is the insertion point for eight muscles in the pelvis. In *mula bandha,* the practitioner engages the pelvic floor in a seal, while retaining the breath after inhalation during *antara kumbhaka.* *Mula bandha* increases the stability of the pelvis and the base of the spine.

To practice *mula bandha,* inhale, and during *antara kumbhaka,* tilt the lower spine gently under and then quickly pull the abdominal muscles, between the pubic bone and navel, inward toward the spine and upward toward the navel. Contract the muscles of the pelvic floor at the site of the perineum, and lift them upward toward the center of the body. The anus will soften and lift inward as well. Suspend the breath. *Mula bandha* redirects the flow of energy in the body from flowing downward to upward so that it can course through the energy channel in the center of the spine and through the chakras. When first practicing *mula bandha,* there may be a sense of squeezing in the perineum, but eventually you will actually feel the contraction deeper within the center of the abdomen. When you practice *mula bandha,* you are really contracting the innermost layer of the pelvic floor, which is a sling of muscles that stretch from the pubic arch, along the side walls of the pelvis and back to the ischial spine. This sling is called the pelvic diaphragm. It is formed by the paired levator ani muscles, which together, form a funnel-shaped muscular floor to the pelvic cavity. The purpose of the pelvic diaphragm is to support the visceral contents of the pelvis. It supports the compressed abdominal viscera during inhalation and is further engaged with the contraction of the abdominal muscles during expiration (Appelman, 1967, 30).

Mula bandha contracts the pelvic diaphragm and lifts the lower abdominal region, creating a platform under the breath, which makes it very interesting to experiment with for singing. *Mula bandha* can assist the singer in engaging the deepest layers of the abdominal muscles for support. For centuries, voice teachers have advocated the engagement of the bottom of the pelvic floor. Many voice teachers have taught students to sing from their genitals or squeeze their anus and buttocks to engage extra support for the voice, especially in the higher registers. Vocal pedagogues now believe that squeezing the lower part of the torso can create unnecessary tension, but practicing *mula bandha* correctly, without undue tension, can assist the singer in gaining awareness of the pelvic diaphragm and a place of deeper support for the voice. Many singers, when they do *mula bandha,* feel that their voice shoots right up into the resonators.

Singing Exercise

Sing, sliding from your lowest note up to your highest note on woooo. Now inhale and engage *mula bandha,* and slide up the scale on woooo again. Did your air move easier? Was it easier to get into the upper registers of the voice?

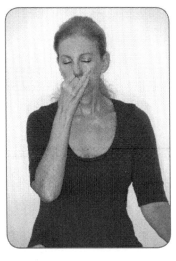

Alternate Nostril Pranayama

For the following exercise, you will use the thumb and the last two fingers of the right hand in a gesture called *pranava mudra*. The fore and middle finger are not to be used. They shall rest folded toward the palm of the hand. This exercise is to be practiced seated with the eyes closed. Keeping the elbow glued to the chest, put the right hand thumb on the right side of the nose and last two fingers on the left side of the nose. By pressing the thumb, the nasal cavity on the right side can be closed, and by pressing the last two fingers, the nasal cavity on the left side can be closed.

Apply light pressure and close the right nostril with the help of the thumb of the right hand. Inhale with the left nostril and exhale through the left nostril. Keep the inhalation smooth and quiet.

Release your thumb, and now close the left nostril by use of the last two fingers of your right hand, and inhale with the right nostril and exhale through the right nostril.

Next, we can alternate breathing. Close the right nostril and inhale with the left nostril. Immediately close the left nostril and exhale with the right nostril. Keeping the left nostril closed, inhale with the right nostril. Immediately close the right nostril and exhale with the left nostril.

After sufficient practice, you can gradually increase the speed at which you inhale and exhale. Do not practice this exercise if you have a headache. Once again, stop the exercise if you feel dizzy or pressure in the head.

Viloma Pranayama

Viloma pranayama requires the practitioner to interrupt inhalation and exhalation. Instead of inhaling or exhaling continuously, the breath stream is interrupted by pausing and holding the breath. You will notice that this exercise is similar to the Tetrazzini exercise.

This exercise can be done lying on your back or seated in a chair, with your eyes closed. There are three parts to this exercise.

Part one: Begin by exhaling all the air out of your lungs. Inhale through the nose for two to three seconds and pause for two or three seconds. Continue to inhale and pause, filling the lungs from the bottom to the top until they are completely full. Keep the abdominal muscles engaged, even during pauses, so that the chest, not the belly, expands with each inhalation. Exhale slowly, without interruption, until the lungs are empty. Repeat for seven to ten minutes.

Part two: Exhale to start, and then inhale slowly through the nose, filling the lungs from the bottom to the top, until they are completely full. Exhale through the nose for two to three seconds and pause, holding back the breath for two or three seconds. Keep exhaling and pausing until the lungs are empty and then repeat the exhalation. Begin with the abdominal muscles engaged to fix the diaphragm and gradually release them, as the chest slowly decreases in size. You may feel a gripping in the diaphragm as it holds back the air from rushing out of the lungs. Repeat for seven to ten minutes.

Part three: Combine both part one and part two. Between the inhalation and exhalation stages of the exercise, do not practice breath retention (*kumbhaka*). Go right into the exhalation stage after the inhalation stage.

A more advanced version of *viloma* pranayama, only recommended for practitioners who have become masters of the previous exercises, is to add breath retention after the inhalation and exhalation stages. *Antara kumbhaka* can be practiced for ten to fifteen seconds after inhalation. *Bahya kumbhaka* can be practiced for five or six seconds after exhalation.

Finally, after the inhalation stage of *viloma* pranayama, you can add the lock *mula bandha* as you suspend your breath in *antara kumbhaka*.

UJJAYI BREATHING

Ujjayi is a pranayama breathing technique that produces a low gentle snoring sound. The yoga practitioner directs a stream of air towards the back of the mouth cavity that slightly constricts the throat and creates a sound.

Inhale through the nose and direct a stream of air to the back of the roof of the mouth and gently constrict the posterior wall of the throat. Make a few fake snoring sounds to feel what part of the back of the mouth cavity is engaged. The throat passage is gently narrowed creating a gentle snoring sound. Some yogis like to think that the sound of *ujjayi* breathing is similar to the gentle rolling waves of the ocean. *Ujjayi* breathing naturally lengthens the breath. Having a surface to direct the air to, on exhalation, can extend and focus the breath. We will discuss this later in the section on resonance. The abdominal muscles and the muscles of the ribcage control the length and speed of the breath. Part of the purpose of *ujjayi* breathing is to strengthen these organs.

There should not be any tension in the vocal cords when you do *ujjayi* breathing. Unfortunately, I have seen many yoga teachers incorrectly teach *ujjayi* breathing. For beginners to yoga, it is often suggested that the *ujjayi* breathing be loud. However, many people create vocal cord tension by squeezing the vocal cords together while trying to produce a loud sound. *Ujjayi* breathing by an experienced practitioner is practically soundless. The skilled practitioner has only a faint sensation of vibration in the throat. *Ujjayi* breathing should cause no vocal distress to the yoga practitioner. If you are experiencing tightness in your throat after practicing *ujjayi* breathing, reduce the volume of sound you produce or stop practicing it altogether for a while.

SHAOLIN BREATHING

Shaolin breathing is a breathing technique from the *Shaolin* monastery in China. Its goal is relaxation and restoration. The first part of the breath exercise is very simple. Gently push your belly out and watch what it does to your breath. The body naturally inhales. Now put your hand on the bottom of your ribcage and open your ribs muscularly. Watch what happens to your breath. You automatically inhale. Also, listen to the breath. You will notice that the inhalation is quiet. Noisy inhalation is a sign of tension somewhere in the throat.

By muscularly opening the ribcage or pushing the belly out, the body will automatically breathe. This information is very comforting to students with performance anxiety who fear that they will not be able to breathe in stressful situations.

The second part of the exercise requires a zafu or a pillow to sit on. Sit cross-legged on the pillow. Put your index finger and thumb together and rest each hand on a knee. Close your eyes and inhale through the nose deeply into your body and rock backwards; exhale through the mouth and rock forward. The torso opens with breath as you inhale and rock backwards, and closes as you rock forward and exhale. Inhalation creates expansion and exhalation contraction. Relax and watch your breath as you rock back and forth. This exercise is very calming and meditative.

BREATHING FOR SOUND PRODUCTION

Now we are going to explore breathing for sound production. You will notice many similarities to yoga pranayama. Breathing can be divided into three categories: clavicular, costal or abdominal. Clavicular breathing is a shallow breath that does not go deeper than the top of the chest. The shoulders will often rise when one takes a clavicular breath. A costal breath is a breath that is initiated by opening the bottom of the ribcage; it is also called a rib-swing breath. A diaphragmatic (abdominal) breath is the deepest breath that one can take; it moves the abdomen outward on inhalation. Herbert Witherspoon (1873-1935), in his book *Singing, A Treatise for Teachers and Students* (1925), called clavicular breathing "the breath of exhaustion," diaphragmatic breathing "the breath of life" and costal or rib breathing "the breath of activity" (1925, 55). He stated that breathing for singing was both diaphragmatic and costal, but costal breathing was "a natural means of obtaining more air for purposes of unusual activity" such as singing. Keeping a high chest position, while singing, directly helps the singer maintain ribcage and waist expansion (1925, 56). Breathing for sound production is different from breathing for everyday life. Most of the time, as we rush through life, we are clavicularly breathing, unconsciously. Vocal pedagogues have long been in agreement that clavicular breathing is not adequate for sound production. For singing or speech, we need to learn to intentionally inhale from a deeper place in the body, so that we can activate certain muscles of the torso to best support sound. Breathing for sound production requires both diaphragmatic and costal (muscles of the ribs) activation. Voice scientist Willard Zemlin, in his book *Speech and Hearing Science, Anatomy and Physiology* (1998), stated that breathing for sound production is both diaphragmatic (abdominal) and intercostal. One does not operate independent of the other (1998, 94).

In many breathing exercises, the student is instructed to put his or her hands on the belly and feel it fill with air. However, there is never any mention of ribcage expansion. For singing or speech, we want to begin with a deep inhalation that fills the belly and also opens the bottom third of the ribcage while expanding the waist 360 degrees. This will enable the lungs to rapidly stretch to their fullest. Your breath may not feel as deep in your abdomen when you add the expansion of the ribs.

The first important step in breathing for sound is to relax the abdominal muscles. According to William Vennard, in his book *Singing: The Mechanism and the Technic,* one of the most difficult things for new singers to learn to do is to relax the abdomen. "Most uninstructed singers, when asked to take a breath, raise the chest, which is good but at the same time they pull the abdomen in so that it cannot move. This forces the organs of the belly up against the diaphragm and makes a deep breath impossible" resulting in a clavicular breath (1967, 29). If you hold your abdominal muscles inward, on inhalation, the diaphragm cannot lower and breathing will be impeded. Pull your belly inward toward the spine and try to take a deep breath. You will notice that you will not be able to do so and you will be forced to breathe in the chest. The deepest layers of your abdominal muscles are attached to the diaphragm, and if they are not relaxed, the diaphragm cannot lower completely. When the abdominal muscles are relaxed, the belly will open outward in response to the diaphragm moving the abdominal viscera out of its way. Some people hold a great deal of tension within their abdomen and are unable to release the abdominal muscles. Others, especially dancers and athletes, overdevelop the abdominals to the point that they are unable to release them. You must be able to relax the abdominal muscles to inhale properly for sound production.

Begin each breath by releasing the belly, allowing it to expand outward and opening the base of the ribcage. Since the diaphragm is attached to the inner surfaces of the ribs, the addition of rib expansion on inhalation also assists the diaphragm in lowering. The belly can open outward and the lower third of the ribcage can expand almost concurrently, but at first it may feel like a two-step process. If we feel the belly open while the ribcage remains closed, we are only allowing the lungs to expand downward and are depriving our body of full breath capacity. We also are not engaging the costal muscles of the ribs, which are important muscles of breath support and vocal power. It is also possible to just belly breathe while maintaining a poor slumped chest posture, which is especially inefficient for singing. Taking a breath while expanding the base of the ribcage requires a "solid" singing posture and helps the singer find the other support muscles of the voice. In the following exercise, we will practice the sensation of intentional breathing. In the abdominal support section, we will learn which muscles support the voice and keep the ribcage engaged in singing.

When we are standing, many of the muscles that we use for breathing are also involved in structural support. Practicing breathing exercises while lying down is a great way for the student to watch the way the body naturally breathes. In this position, the breath naturally drops to the core of the body and the chest stays lifted. The goal of the singer is to be able to breathe in this manner when standing.

Exercise

Lie on your back and put one hand on the belly and the other hand on the side of the base of the ribcage. Inhale and feel how the belly lifts upward and the base of the ribcage opens naturally. If you don't feel the base of your ribcage expand, find the very bottom rib just above the side of your belly. When you breathe you will feel this rib move. Many people are unaware of movement in the ribcage during inhalation but, when instructed to find it, can feel the ribcage open laterally and the front of the ribs lift up. It is advantageous to have movement of both the front, lateral and back ribs. This is not always experienced at first, due to each person's individual costal flexibility. If you have little mobility of the back ribs, try the back rib exercise that follows and, if you have little mobility in the side ribs, try the spinal twist exercise. Continue to breathe, feeling the belly and rib movement. Notice how delicious and calming it feels to become aware of the body's natural, graceful core dance.

THE TENTH RIB

Acclaimed vocal expert Richard Miller (1926-2009) said that breathing for sound production is all about awareness of the tenth rib (199, 240). The tenth ribs are the very bottom ribs that attach to the front of the ribcage and sternum. We have two more ribs, ribs eleven and twelve, that are called floating ribs. These ribs do not attach to the ribcage in the front; they originate at the thoracic spine and end at the sides of the waist, thus floating outside the abdominal viscera. You can feel these ribs in your back. If you dig your fingers deeply into the sides of the back of your waist, you will feel their bony protrusions.

Lie down on your back and put your hands on your waist with your index finger on the tenth ribs in the front of your body and your thumbs on your floating ribs in the back of your waist. Release your belly and inhale while expanding the base of the ribcage and waist. Notice that the whole circumference of your waist increases. The singer's goal is to be able to keep this area expanded while singing. Exhale and notice that your ribs and waist return to their pre-inhalation position. Inhalation expands the waist and exhalation decreases the waist. Continue practicing until you have awareness of movement in your core and can maintain it in a different posture.

Slowly roll to one side while still focusing on the rib and waist movement. Slowly sit up, still focusing on the movement. See if you can rise to a standing position while still feeling the base of your ribcage and waist expanding. Notice the tendency to hold the breath while moving. Most of us have become disconnected and unaware of the sensation of diaphragmatic deep breathing, which causes movement in the core of the body. If you are a habitual shallow breather or breath holder, the habit you have acquired may be difficult to break. By practicing diaphragmatic breathing, your body will learn a new behavior that it will actually like. Also, if you are a person who suffers from anxiety or panic attacks, doing diaphragmatic breathing can calm your nervous system. Psychologists often instruct their patients to do deep breathing exercises during anxiety attacks. However, someone who is having a panic attack may not be able to tell if he or she is actually breathing deeply. By focusing on the sensation of the ribcage and waist expanding, you are automatically breathing deeply and diaphragmatically. This results in relaxation of the body and mind.

CHEST POSITION FOR SINGING

Put one hand on your breastbone and another on the side of the bottom of your ribcage and inhale. Notice that the chest lifts on inhalation and the sides of the ribcage open. Hold the chest up by using the muscles of the chest, keeping the shoulders and neck relaxed, and notice that the base of the ribcage does not close. There is a direct correlation between the position of the chest and the expansion of the base of the ribcage. Exhale and notice that the chest lowers and the ribcage closes as you run out of air. In singing, we want to remain in the position of inhalation as long as we can, and one of the easiest ways to do that is to keep the chest lifted at all times. Remember, the position of inhalation is achieved when the base of your ribcage and waist are expanded. Standing in a posture with an elevated chest and maintaining a high chest position, throughout a song, directly helps the singer maintain ribcage and waist expansion (Appelman, 1967, 14). The chest does not drop even when breathing in between phrases. The high chest position makes the replenishing of air very quick and barely visible to the audience. Keeping the chest up may be difficult for people with poor posture at first, but the muscles of the torso will become stronger through practice, and eventually the singer can comfortably keep the chest lifted.

MOUTH BREATHING

Breathe through the mouth in all of these exercises unless otherwise instructed. We rarely have the time to nose breathe in singing or stage speech, so we must master mouth breathing. To see how much time nose breathing takes, sing a fast song and nose breathe between phrases. Notice that nose breathing will take too long and the rhythm of the song will be interrupted.

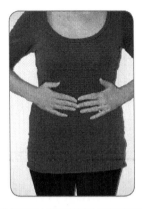

WAIST EXPANSION EXERCISE

Put your hands at waist level at the base of the front of your ribcage. Find the very bottom rib on each side of the ribcage and rest your index fingers on these ribs. Let your index and middle fingers of each hand touch. Take a breath and notice that your fingers no longer touch as the base of your ribcage and your waist expands on inhalation. Exhale and let your fingers come back together as the waist and ribcage return to their original position.

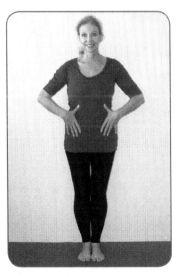

BELLY DANCE ISOLATIONS

Some people have little awareness of their ribcage as a separate entity from the rest of the torso. This exercise is a belly dance exercise that will give the student the awareness of the size and shape and possible mobility of the ribcage.

Without moving the hips, lift the front of the ribcage upward and out of the waist. Use your front abdominal muscles to lift the chest. Try moving the ribcage from one side to the other. Then try moving the ribcage out to the front and then to the back. Now try making a circle with the ribcage; move it to the front, to the side, to the back and to the other side, still without moving the hips.

SPINAL TWIST

This exercise helps you gain flexibility in the ribcage on both sides of the body. Lie on your back. Bring your knees up to your chest and let them fall to the side as close to your armpit as possible. Reach the opposite arm along the ground up

toward your ear. Breathe into your side ribs that are now stretched open toward the ceiling. See if you can breathe all the way up into the armpit, letting breath stretch the muscles between your ribs. Do the other side.

SEATED TWIST

Sit cross-legged or in half lotus on the floor. Put your right hand on your left knee and your left hand on the floor behind you as you twist to the left. Keep your chin parallel to the ground and let the head follow the twist of the torso. Then, lift your left arm up in the air and arch your body over your right knee as you look up. Hold the stretch and breathe into the left side of your ribcage. See if you can get the breath to open the costal muscles between the ribs that are facing toward the ceiling. Do the other side.

BACK OPENING EXERCISE

The back is able to expand during inhalation, but many of us have little sensation of this. This exercise will help your posterior ribcage gain flexibility and increase your breathing awareness of the potential of the back as a breathing place. Come into the yoga

posture child's pose on the ground or sit in a chair and bend over. Breathe and see if you can feel the back of the base of the ribcage open. See if you can separate your kidneys with breath. Breathe in on a count of five, suspend your breath for a count of five and exhale on five. Increase the count. You can also lift your arms up toward the ceiling, further stretching the top of your back.

BOLSTER BREATHING

A bolster is a long cylinder used in yoga to lie on. You can make a bolster out of two Mexican blankets, regular blankets or beach towels. You can also order bolsters from yoga product sites on the Internet. Iyengar yoga is fond of

using Mexican blankets because they are soft and inexpensive. Roll up your blankets or towels tightly until you make a bolster about eight inches in diameter and 14 to 16 inches long. Put the bolster lengthwise on your yoga mat and sit down at one end of the bolster. Lay your back and head down on the bolster and spread your arms open to the side and relax. The bolster supports your spine but allows the shoulders to fall open and release to the ground, giving the upper back a nice release. If your lower back hurts in this posture, make your bolster thinner.

In this posture, notice how your abdominal muscles are stretched. Let's explore belly breathing in this posture. Breathe into your belly, feeling the belly rise and fall, but don't let the ribcage open. Now, let's do the opposite and explore ribcage breathing. Breathe into the sides of your ribs, allowing the ribcage to open, but do not let the breath open into the belly. Let's do a four-count breathing exercise. Counting in your head, inhale into the bottom of your abdomen on the count of one, bring the breath up into the bottom of the ribcage on two, up into the chest on the count of three and up to the collarbone on four, then exhale. Feel the costal muscles between the ribs stretch with each inhalation. Ribcage flexibility is important for good respiratory health, so this is a wonderful exercise to stretch the muscles of the ribs. This is also a wonderful restorative exercise to do after a long day, especially if it has been spent bent over a desk!

SQUAT BREATHING

If you are able to get down onto the ground in a yoga squat position, this is a really fun yoga posture to breathe and sound in. Only do this posture with your feet on the ground if you can do it without pain in your feet or calves. This posture requires a lot of flexibility in the calf muscles and tendons of the ankle. You can also do an alternative squat posture, if you have tight

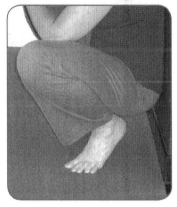

ankles and calves, against a wall. Lean your back against a wall and slide down into a squat position, keeping your back against the wall. Don't stay too long in this posture, just as long as feels comfortable. Feel free to put your hands on the ground in front of you in either posture, to balance if necessary. Breathe and notice how you can feel your breath coming all the way from the pelvic floor and buttocks. Voice coach Patsy Rodenburg, in her book *The Actor Speaks,* suggests singing or speaking text in this posture (2008, 44). You will feel your voice deeply root in the body. This posture is especially good for singing the blues or speaking low notes.

BEGINNING SUNRISE SALUTATION EXERCISE

The sunrise salutation exercise is a warm-up exercise from yoga that begins with the yogi stretching the arms up and overhead. This is a great posture to open and stretch the ribcage. By opening the lower ribcage, the student can breathe from the depths of the lungs and feel air under the ribcage.

Stand upright, with your feet shoulder distance apart, with arms at your sides, palms on your thighs, and breathe through the mouth. Rotate your hands so the palms face outward; inhale and raise your hands upward, stretching the arms outward until they meet overhead touching palm to palm. Take three full breaths, breathing through the mouth, and see if you can feel the breath in the space under the ribcage. Rotate your hands so they touch overhead, back of hand to back of hand. Take three more breaths and notice the change in the ribcage. Most people experience more opening in the back of their ribcage. Take a fourth breath and exhale, lowering your arms back to your sides, but do not let the ribs drop all the way down quickly. Let them float down. Many singers, due to poor posture, sink their chest into their hips. After exhaling, see if you can retain a position of the ribcage gently floating out of the waist, and try singing.

TETRAZZINI EXERCISE

These were the favorite breathing exercises of the great opera singer of the nineteenth century, Luisa Tetrazzini (1871-1940), which she dictated for the book, *Caruso and Tetrazzini on Singing* in 1909 (1909, 12). For this exercise you will breathe through your nose and exhale through your mouth. This is a fantastic exercise to become aware of the expansion and contraction of the ribcage during breathing. It also teaches the singer how to slow down exhalation so that the recoil forces of the ribcage do not take over.

Part one: Stand erect and imagine the lungs are empty sacks (we know this is not true but imagine this to be so). Inhale and imagine that the air is dropping into the lungs like a weight, first filling the bottom of the lungs, then the middle and then the top. Exhale.

Part two: Inhale air through the nostrils in little puffs. Take a very little bit of air at a time and feel as if you are filling the very bottom and back of the lungs. When you have the sensation of being full up to the neck, retain the air for a few seconds and then, very slowly, send it out in little puffs through the mouth. It can help to purse the lips while you exhale. Notice that the ribcage opens and closes in stages relative to your breath.

FARINELLI EXERCISE

Carlo Broschi, called Farinelli (1705-1782), was one of the last great castrati singers. Music historians have found many references in old opera reviews, hailing his amazing breath control. This is the exercise that he swore gave him his legendary breath capacity. Inhale through the mouth, counting in your mind to five, expanding the whole base of the ribcage and the abdominal region. Suspend (don't inhale or exhale) while you mentally count to five, without closing the glottis (the opening between the vocal cords) or squeezing the throat. Slowly exhale while you mentally count to five. Notice if any tension creeps into your neck or shoulders during the suspension phase of this exercise. If it does, rotate the neck and shoulders while you are holding your breath. Gradually increase your count all the way to 10.

Inhale	Suspend	Exhale
12345-------------------	12345-------------------	12345
123456-----------------	123456-----------------	123456
1234567----------------	1234567----------------	1234567

Add counting out loud. Do the exercise again and when you are at the suspend stage of the exercise, relax the throat and count out loud, first to five and then consecutively up to ten. A little air may come out with each number that you count out loud, so you may not have as much air left over during the exhalation part of the exercise (Miller, 2004, 6).

RIBCAGE STRENGTH

Gaining control of ribcage descent is of supreme importance to anyone who wants to expand his or her breath control. One of the goals of the actor and the singer is to have control of the ribcage and to be able to hold it open if necessary, or control its descent. However, most untrained singers, actors or speakers will not have enough strength in their ribcage muscles (costal muscles) to do this. By controlling the descent of the ribcage, together with the abdominal muscles, the singer or actor controls the emission of the breath stream.

Some of the old Italian exercises for strengthening the ribcage appear to be rather torturous to the singer.

Some voice teachers used abdominal belts in their voice teaching. They would have a student inhale and then they would tie a belt around the base of the ribcage and upper abdomen of the student, and require the student to sing, without letting the belt drop, thus requiring the student to keep his or her ribcage and abdomen expanded. By having to muscularly hold the ribcage open, the student developed costal, abdominal and back muscle strength.

Giovanni Sbriglia (1832-1916) was a celebrated Neapolitan opera singer and teacher who some historians believe created the Paris School of Singing. He was the inventor of the abdominal belt. He said, "The foundation of my teaching is perfect breath control without tension . . . a high chest held high without tension by developed abdominal and lower back muscles and a straight spine" (Coffin, 1989, 99).

Belt Exercise

Go ahead and get a belt and tie it around your upper abdomen and the base of your ribcage and speak or sing, seeing if you can keep the ribcage flexed. Some theatrical voice methods require the actor to keep his or her ribcage flexed open at all times; this is called rib-reserve. Opera singers use rib-reserve to hold back the large volume of breath required to produce intense sound. I don't advocate rib-reserve for speech, as I think it can cause unnecessary tension, but I think some of the exercises that would enable the student to have the strength for rib-reserve are beneficial. Let's take a look at some more of the historical breathing exercises to train the breath.

Opera Hands Position Exercise

Many opera singers sang with their hands clasped in front of their chest at breast level to activate extra support for the voice. By clasping their hands at breast level, they were able to keep the ribcage lifted and activate the costal muscles.

One of the reasons for holding the hands together was to activate the *point d'appui*. Giovanni Sbriglia's method of breath control was to focus the breath, during exhalation, against what he called the *point d'appui*. The *point d'appui* was a focal point in the chest that, he said, was the major place of support.

"[As you sing] the air is slowly pushed out of the body through the small bronchial tubes, which merge into the big bronchial tube at the focal point in the chest . . . the *point d'appui*—the place of support, the place where everything rests . . ." (Coffin, 1989, 99).

This method became very popular. The famous opera singer Luisa Tetrazzini, while singing, liked to press her chest against her clasped hands, and direct her breath toward her chest, which she said increased the activity of support of the chest and ribcage (1909, 12). By directing the breath toward the chest, the ribcage stayed expanded and held back the rushing of air against the vocal cords, allowing the singer to keep his or her throat relaxed. This method is still used today, most frequently in recital performances.

Let's try this exercise. Clasp your hands together in front of your body, palm to palm, and raise them up to chest level. Keep your elbows elevated and gently press your palms together; see if you can raise the sides of the ribcage. Easy does it, too much pressing of the palms together can create tension in the neck and shoulders. Now sing a long "ah." Do you have more vocal power?

MANUAL GARCIA II EXERCISE

Manuel Garcia II (1805-1906) is considered the father of voice science. He was the inventor of the laryngoscope. The laryngoscope is a small mirror with a long metal handle that can be inserted into the mouth for observation of the vocal cords. This instrument is still widely used today.

Garcia II's father, Garcia I (1775-1832), was also a famous voice teacher. He advocated an erect standing posture for singing with the shoulders back and the hands crossed behind the lower back, with the palms facing outward. Garcia I claimed it would "open the chest and bring out the voice" (Coffin, 1989, 16). This posture became known as the "Garcia posture" and is still in use today. It is also called the "noble posture."

Garcia II's method of inspiration was one of both diaphragmatic lowering and ribcage expansion. He wrote of the act of respiration as being a two-part process, beginning with the diaphragm lowering and the stomach slightly protruding. He called this abdominal breathing and stated that this is only a partial breath.

"During this partial inspiration . . . the ribs do not move, nor are they filled to their full capacity, to obtain which the diaphragm must and does contract completely. Then and only then are the ribs raised, while the stomach is drawn in" (1982, 4).

Garcia stated that a complete breath is not achieved until the ribs freely expand 360 degrees. "This inspiration is complete and is called thoracic or intercostal" (1982, 4).

"This double procedure, on which I insist, enlarges the lungs, first at the base, then by the circumference, and allows the lungs to complete all their expansion and to receive all the air which they can contain. To advise abdominal breathing exclusively would be to voluntarily reduce by one half the element of strength most indispensable to the singer, the breath" (1847, 184).

Garcia II created his own breathing exercises to strengthen the lungs for singing. He said that since the lungs were independent of the vocal organs, breathing exercises would not create voice fatigue. In *Hints on Singing* (second edition), he suggested the following (1982, 5):

1. Draw a breath slowly through a very minute opening of the lips, then exhale freely.

2. Breathe freely and exhale slowly through the same small opening.

3. Breathe freely and retain the breath during ten seconds or more.

THE WHISPERED AH

"The beauty of singing demands a complete mastery over the breath in order to preserve the natural openness of the throat," stated William Shakespeare (the singing teacher not the playwright) in his book *Plain Words on Singing* (1924, 3). William Shakespeare (1849-1931) was a student of Francesco Lamperti, one of the fathers of voice technique. He attempted to write down in his book the techniques of the Italian masters that were only passed down orally from teacher to student. In his book, Shakespeare very effectively describes the process that the Italian singing masters used to develop breath control. He stated that the singer should begin with exercises on a "whispered ah." "The act of breathing out slowly should be like warming, quite different from that of blowing," stated Shakespeare (1924, 8). The tendency for a new student is to blow air instead of gradually releasing air from the lungs. By first learning to control a whisper of breath while imagining the notes, the singer will learn to not tighten the throat, tongue or jaw. Then the student can add sound to the exercises and hopefully keep the tongue, jaw and throat fully released. F.M. Alexander, the creator of Alexander Technique, adapted this Italian singing technique for speech and also called his exercise "the whispered ah."

Put your hand against your mouth and blow air hard. Notice

how quickly air is expelled from the lungs and what muscles are activated in your torso, throat, tongue and jaw. Blowing air requires the constriction of either the lips or the throat. Put your hand against your mouth again and slowly let your air out so that it warms your hand. Notice how different this feels in your body and which muscles in your core are activated to control the slow outflow of breath. While warming the hand with air, the throat should remain open and relaxed, with no need to engage the tongue or the jaw. Learning to control the breath while keeping the throat, tongue and jaw relaxed is the goal of the singer. The "whispered ah" exercises below are some of my favorite exercises to achieve this goal.

Different pitches and intensities require different levels of breath pressure. By first practicing on the "whispered ah," the singer can learn to control the outflow of breath as well as regulate a variety of air pressures while maintaining a relaxed throat, tongue and jaw. Shakespeare advised "that you are not to sing louder or bigger than the controlled breath at command warrants, and that you must try to finish each phrase with a note to spare, which, of course, need not be sung" (1924, 23). The tendency for many singers is to try to push the voice beyond what the singer can control. Shakespeare said that his teacher Francesco Lamperti always said, "The breath of a good note should feel as if it comes towards one" (1924, 9). Put your hand in front of your mouth again and try warming it while imagining that you are inhaling instead of exhaling, as if the note is coming toward you instead of leaving your mouth. Many singers feel that they don't push and have more breath if they use this visualization.

The following exercises are all William Shakespeare's excellent exercises for breath control. He suggested that you inhale through the mouth for all of these exercises. He felt it took too long to inhale through the nose.

Fifteen Seconds Exercise

In this exercise, exhale on an easy whispered "ah" for fifteen seconds. Make the whispered "ah" barely audible, keeping the throat and tongue completely relaxed. This whispered "ah" is different than the type of whisper you might use as quiet speech. It will not fatigue the vocal cords. Notice if you try to tighten your throat or engage your tongue, neither of which is necessary as you are only exhaling on an "ah." Do the exercise again and imagine that you are inhaling the "ah" and see if you feel like you have more control over your breath (1924, 21).

Air Pressure Exercise

Whisper an "ah" for ten seconds. In the first five seconds, use a gentle, easy air pressure and then, in the last five seconds, increase the air pressure but still keep the throat, tongue and jaw relaxed, unaffected by the increase of air pressure.

Staccato Ahs

Practice five staccato "ahs," first on the whispered "ah" and then on a comfortable speech level tone, only breathing at the end of the group of five. Shakespeare felt that the practice of staccato notes was very effective in training the breath. He also suggested that you should feel that you are "talking on the vowel" and that "it would be well, always mentally to associate some word or idea with the 'ah'" (1924, 28).

Whisper an "ah"   ah ah ah ah ah, breathe
Sing an "ah"   ah ah ah ah ah, breathe
Then alternate between "ah" and "oh"
Start to add an ascending major scale after the five staccato "ahs"

Counting: Do the same exercise, but instead of exhaling on a sighing "whispered ah," count out loud (1924, 22). Count backwards starting on nineteen, humming on the [n]. See if you can control the floating down of the ribs and the closing of the waistline so that the ribcage and waist return to their pre-inhalation position on one. Now do the exercise again. Can you count down to one but still keep some sense of expansion in the base of the ribcage and the waist? Shakespeare suggested that you always end a phrase with some notes to spare; once the ribcage and waist return to the state of complete exhalation, there will be no breath left to continue singing. You can also count out loud, starting on one, and then going as far as you can. Be sure to hum on the [n]. Try this exercise imagining that the notes are coming toward you or that you are inhaling the notes. I bet you will be able to count further. Shakespeare recommended that you learn to be able to count to forty on one breath.

Song on Whispered Ah

Pick a song you want to learn and sing the whole song on a "whispered ah." You will be imagining the notes. Notice if there are any parts of the song where you feel that you lose the sensation of a relaxed throat, tongue and jaw. Keep practicing until you can sing that part of the song without unnecessary tension. Were you forcing your breath in that part of the song? Now sing the song again with actual tone on an "ah" and see if your throat, tongue and jaw can remain unchanged even though you are now engaging the vocal cords. Finally add the words to the song.

WILLIAM SHAKESPEARE'S EXERCISE

William Shakespeare suggested in *The Art of Singing* (1910) that breathing include the raising of the ribs in the back. He wrote that the muscles "which join the ribs to the backbone and the spine are that on which the singer must chiefly rely in order to raise the ribs during inspiration" (1910, 13). This resulted in expansion of the back, but little chest expansion. Shakespeare's idea of back breathing caused considerable back spreading and is not considered good vocal pedagogy today, but the exercise is interesting to experiment with.

"Half fill the lungs through the mouth and then breathe in and out small amounts of air quickly and noiselessly until you feel yourself panting, yet doing nothing with the chest and without filling the lungs. Now extend this quick, noiseless panting or quivering until it is felt not only at the soft place but at the sides and near the shoulder blades. Then go to a full breath and pronounce a long ah for ten or fifteen seconds" (1910, 16).

RIBCAGE PULSES

Put your hands on the base of each side of your ribcage. Using just the costal muscles, inhale and muscularly pull the base of your ribcage out to the sides in little pulses. Now silently count one, two, three and four as you pulse your ribcage outward. You are stretching and strengthening the costal muscles.

When we are in complete exhalation, there is a little bit of residual air still in the lungs that we can force out to poor results.

SIBILANT S EXERCISE

This is an old singing exercise to engage the abdominal support for the voice and learn to expel air from the lungs at a slow continuous pace. Try this exercise lying on your back. Since the support muscles of the voice are also muscles of posture, it can be more difficult to isolate them while standing.

Put one hand on the side of your lower ribcage and the other on your belly. Inhale and slowly exhale on an ssss hiss like a snake. Exhale as slowly as you can, noticing how the ribcage very slowly descends and the abdominal muscles under your hand go in as you start to run out of breath. Extend the breath for as long as you can and see what happens to the abdominal muscles as you are running out of air. You will feel your belly pull in toward your spine. Now do the same exercise but instead of exhaling on ssss, exhale on a shhhh. Now try a zzzz. Many people find that when they add tone to the sound they don't have as much breath. Go back to exhaling on an ssss hiss and then try a zzzz sound and see if you can extend the breath on the zzzz longer. You can try this exercise standing after you have experienced it lying down. Were you able to control your breath release easier lying down or standing?

UMBRELLA EXERCISE

The umbrella analogy has sometimes been used in voice work to describe the ribcage. Imagine the ribcage as an umbrella, closed on the sides but open on the bottom. The lungs are housed inside the umbrella, and as the umbrella expands, so do the lungs. Get an umbrella, and if you aren't superstitious about opening an umbrella inside, inhale and slowly open the umbrella at the same time, almost all the way, but don't lock it open. Open the umbrella slowly to coincide with the opening of your ribcage. Exhale slowly, pacing the closing of your ribcage with the closing of the umbrella. Do not close the umbrella, or your ribcage, completely until you have finished the phrase and need to take another breath. We want to learn to control the descent of the ribcage in the same way that an umbrella closes. When the ribcage is completely closed, the singer or speaker is in compete exhalation and any phonation at this point will cause tension in the throat or body since the singer or speaker is out of breath. To keep making sound, the singer or speaker must force or squeeze the air out of the body, which usually results in squeezing the ribcage inward and tension in the vocal cords.

Now do the exercise again using text or a song phrase and coordinate the closing of the ribcage with the pace of the phrase. Keep the ribcage open as long as it feels comfortable and then control its descent. Make sure you finish the phrase before your ribcage completely closes. Just a nanosecond of leaving the ribcage open will keep the last word of a phrase supported.

PRAYER HANDS

You can also do this exercise with your hands. Put your hands in a prayer position out in front of your chest. Keeping the fingertips together, move the palms of your hands out toward the side and inhale, expanding the base of your ribcage and waist at the same time as your hands open.

NO BREATH EXERCISE

Many singers, actors and public speakers forget to breathe before sounding. Don't take a breath and sing an ahhh [a] for as long as you can. What does that feel like? When we are in complete exhalation, there is a little bit of residual air still in the lungs that we can force out to poor results. Sometimes we can get away with sounding without inhalation, but more often, the result of sounding on residual air will be immediate tension in the larynx and squeezing in the ribs. Unfortunately, many beginning singers and speakers sometimes do this until they get in the habit of breathing deeply for sound. So, developing good breathing habits is very important for healthy voice use.

THE CATCH BREATH EXERCISE

Sometimes in a song, speech or monologue, singers, speakers and actors have only a second to breathe between words. Therefore, they must learn to master the catch breath. A catch breath is a very fast breath that can be undetected by an audience. The catch breath is a quiet mouth breath that opens the base of the ribcage and abdomen quickly. Put each of your thumbs on the bottom front of your ribcage. Take two quick, small, quiet inhalations (ha ha), expanding the abdomen above the navel and the bottom of the ribcage concurrently. Now try to do the same thing with one fast inhalation. The sensation can sometimes feel like you are taking in a quick small gulp of air. These quick breaths will almost resemble a fast pant. Hang your tongue out of your mouth and pant. Pant faster and faster. You will notice that the base of the ribcage and abdominal area open quickly. If you keep panting, the line between inhalation and exhalation can become blurred. The bodies of well-trained singers learn to replenish air as automatically as you feel your air replenishing in this exercise. That is why it can be difficult to see the visible act of inhalation in well-trained singers.

William Vennard, in his book *Singing: The Mechanism and the Technic* (1967), recommended that the singer use a "surprise breath." He suggested that the singer take a breath and imagine being pleasantly surprised. "The 'surprise' breath not only is quick and deep, but it also, by reflex action, usually produces the best adjustment of the throat" (1967, 35).

Try taking a catch breath as you did before, but this time, act as if you have just been surprised. The first breath you take may make a gasping sound. If so, do the exercise again and, this time, make the inhalation quiet. You may need to relax your throat to assist in a quiet inhalation.

FOUR WORST HABITS OF BREATHING

Beginning students of voice work can sometimes develop bad breathing habits. The first worst habit of breathing we call "the hesitation." This is when you breathe in, hold your breath and then speak or sing, a classic form of hesitation.

Hesitating by holding the breath before speaking or singing can cause the vocal cords to close, creating immediate vocal cord and throat tension before you have uttered a sound. Always go directly from inhalation to sound production. Don't wait to let tension creep in.

The second worst breathing habit we call "the poor follow-through." Voice teachers see this problem frequently in beginning students. The student takes a good inhalation, but starts to speak or sing quickly before connecting the voice to the support muscles of the body. In "the poor follow-through," instead of remaining in the position of inhalation, the student immediately lets the ribcage slam shut, drops the abdominal breath support, and then proceeds to speak or sing in the posture of complete exhalation. All the advantages of good breathing are instantly lost, and the student will run out of air quickly and have no support for the voice. Students must gain the awareness of what it is like to make sound with support from the core of the body, and not sing or speak until they feel this support. If you have this problem, best to go back to the ribcage exercises and practice them some more. The Tetrazzini, lip buzzes and the sibilant ssss exercises are especially helpful.

The third poorest habit of breathing is to breathe in, feel the breath support, but not be able to stay connected to it through a complete phrase, resulting in a decline in vocal power. This habit is similar to the previous habit of poor follow-through, but often has to do with the inability of the singer to pace his or her exhalation and keep the breath energized until the end of the phrase. Singing or speech requires energy, and as the singer or speaker runs out of air, he or she will have to increase energy. This is also caused by lack of training of the ribcage and abdominal support muscles. In speaking, lack of breath support through a whole phrase can cause the last word to drop off and be unheard. In singing, lack of breath support can result in the last note of a phrase being flat or out of tune. This is a common occurrence in pop singing today.

The fourth poor habit of breathing is laziness. The student doesn't practice vocal exercises. The breath muscles weaken within days of not working. Therefore, it is necessary to practice breathing exercises regularly. A new singer, public speaker or actor has to gain control of strong reflexes in the body that need to be retrained for sound production, so frequent practice is required.

THE VOCAL CORDS

Our lungs are composed of a network of small tubes called bronchi that merge into larger tubes, and finally into one tube, called the windpipe or trachea, that leads the air from the lungs, through the vocal cords and into the mouth. Vocal scientists now believe that

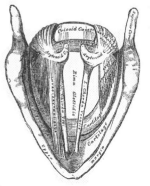

the trachea vibrates when we sing. The vocal cords are housed within the thyroid cartilage of the larynx (Adam's apple), which sits on top of the cricoid cartilage at the top of the trachea (windpipe). They come together, in vibration, when we speak or sing. The vocal cords, also called vocal folds, are not actually cords but two folds of tissue called the thyroarytenoid muscles. They are attached to two triangle shaped cartilages (arytenoid cartilages) that pull the vocal folds together over the air passage (glottis), causing them to vibrate and produce speech or singing. The very edges of the vocal folds are composed of a thin ligament. Parallel to the ligament lies the vocalis muscle, which is the vibrating mass of the thyroarytenoid muscle that produces sound. The vocal cords are longer in a man, creating a lower pitched sound than the sound that is made by a woman's shorter vocal cords. A man's vocal cords are between 17 mm to 25 mm in length (.66 to .98 of an inch). A woman's vocal cords are between 12.5 mm and 17.5 mm (.49 to .68 of an inch). So, a human's vocal cords are actually quite small, which is amazing considering all the fantastic sounds we can make with them. Changes in pitch occur due to variation in the length, tension and mass of the vocal cords.

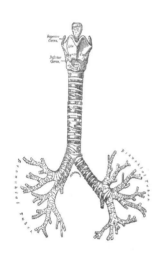

Our instrument is a long tube with a set of vocal cords on top that act like lips, that are able to make a variety of pitches. They are only a small vibrating part of an instrument that is much larger. The vocal cords are never to be used as the power source for the voice. Any attempt at powering the voice from the vocal cords will stop the rhythm of their vibration and create tension in them, creating an unpleasant sensation and corruption of tone. Since we all know that our vocal cords are in our throat, the throat is the first place we will try to use for power until we have some training. Continued singing or speaking using the vocal cords as the power source for the voice can cause vocal polyps, nodules and hemorrhages. Therefore, it is of the utmost importance that anyone who is serious about singing, acting or speaking seeks out professional training.

BABY BREATHING

Have you ever watched a baby breathe? The whole torso moves when they breathe. They also have no problem screaming and crying from the core of the body for a long time. If you watch babies cry, their whole bodies are engaged in the process of making sound. Their voice does not emit just from their neck and mouth, with the rest of

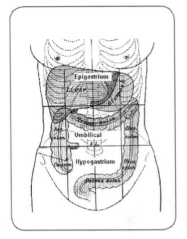

the body appearing still and disconnected from the voice. Their whole body is engaged in the making of sound. They breathe from their armpits all the way down to their hips and, when sounding, they like to arch their back and stretch the whole front of their torso as support for the sound.

Lie on your back and relax and breathe, noticing the movement in the ribs and the belly. Notice how you don't have to really think about breathing from the center of your body when you are lying down; the breath just naturally goes into the belly and lower rib cage. When we are standing or sitting up, the spine, ribcage and muscles of the torso are actively involved in structural support. They can also be holding all of the tensions that accompany us as we move through life. It can be difficult for us to breathe from our core and to isolate the support muscles for the voice when standing, due to postural tensions. When we are lying down, the only job the ribcage, spine and abdominal muscles have is to assist us in breathing and sounding, so it is much easier to isolate specific muscle sensations for the voice in a supine posture.

After relaxing and watching your breathing, gently roll over until you are lying on your belly. You should be able to feel your breath right under you, in your epigastric, umbilical and hypogastric (area from

the base of your sternum to your pubic bone) regions (see photo). Now with your lips closed, make an mmm mmm sound on any comfortable mid-range pitch in your speaking register and see if you can get your belly to move and vibrate with the sound. See if you can feel the sound starting from deep within your core. What you are feeling is the connection of your voice to the abdominal muscles.

Once you can get your abdominal muscles to vibrate with sound, see if you can vocalize a chant on the words, my-yoh my-yoh, using the same comfortable mid-range pitch you used before, still keeping the sensation of the connection of the voice to the abdominal muscles. It will feel like there is a gentle humming vibration in your belly.

The next stage is to move onto your forearms, still keeping your belly on the ground like a baby begins to do when it can start to pull itself up. Feel your lower ribcage and belly expand on inhalation and hum mm to my-yoh my-yoh until you have a clear sensation of the voice vibrating in your abdomen under you. If you

don't feel your voice sounding in your core when lying completely down, this position can be easier as you are balancing right on the belly and, therefore, right on the abdominal muscles. The next stage in a baby's

development is to crawl. So, slowly, paying great attention to your breathing and toning on my-yoh my-yoh, see if you can still keep the sensation of your voice vibrating in your abdominal muscles as you get onto your hands and knees.

The next stage is to sit back onto your heels and still feel the vibration of your voice in your core, and lastly, come to a full standing position while still keeping the connection of the voice to the abdominal muscles. Rise to a standing position very slowly, paying attention to your breathing and keeping the sensation of the sound in the abdominal muscles.

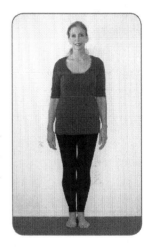

If you find that you have lost the sensation of the voice in the abdominal muscles, then go back down onto your belly and do the process again. Has your breathing changed now that you are standing? Many students find that, when standing, they lose the sensation of the voice in their core.

Don't skip any of the stages: stage one: flat on belly; stage two: pull up onto forearms; stage three: onto hands and knees; stage four: sitting on heels; and stage five: standing. You might even want to go to kneeling before standing. Only go as far as you can while still being aware of the vibration of your voice in your core. You might only make it onto all fours at first, before you lose the sensation, or have to remain on your belly for some time.

The next step is to try this exercise on other sounds. Try "woo woo," "voom voom" and "zooba zooba." Try chanting while counting. Eventually try a song, keeping the humming vibration alive in your core.

Practice this exercise over and over. It will help you gain awareness of the subtle sense of vibration of sound in your core, which takes time for a singer or speaker to develop.

Let's take a look at where the power of the voice is and learn techniques to reorganize the body into a system of supported sounding that is safe, healthy and natural.

> *Some yogis like to think that the sound of ujjayi breathing is similar to the gentle rolling waves of the ocean.*

Part Two

FINDING YOUR VOICE

Definition of support: The voice is supported when the abdominal musculature is actively controlling the exhalation of the airstream.

Chapter Five

ABDOMINAL SUPPORT MUSCLES

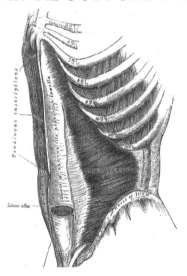

MUSCLES OF SUPPORT

MANY SINGERS AND ACTORS WILL hear the expression, "support the voice," from voice teachers, choir directors and acting instructors. Unfortunately, many teachers do not clearly explain what this means. I did not fully understand what "support the voice" meant until I studied abdominal anatomy and physiology and the role of the muscles of expiration. Therefore, I have presented in this chapter an overview of the major muscles of expiration. There is a direct relationship between the engagement of the abdominal musculature and the voice, with the voice being supported when the abdominal musculature is actively controlling the exhalation of the airstream.

The singer or speaker should have a clear sensation of the abdominal muscles actively engaged in the core when using the voice at all times. Without the use of the abdominal musculature to support the voice, the singer or speaker will have immediate tension in the throat and will not use the voice efficiently.

Although when we sing we do many acrobatic feats with our voice, singing is simply a matter of delaying exhalation. Delayed exhalation occurs when the abdominal musculature and muscles of the thoracic cage actively slow down the expulsion of air.

According to voice scientist D. Ralph Appelman (1908-1993) in his book, *The Science of Vocal Pedagogy* (1967), "Support is the act of constantly sustaining the vocalized sound by use of the breath pressure" (1967, 11). Appelman expands on this concept in the following paragraph:

"The singer must conceive of the act of expiration in a song as one of balanced suspension, with the muscles of inspiration, the rib raisers, acting as antagonists and the muscles of expiration acting as the control muscles which supply an even pressure in the expulsion of air" (1967, 37).

The diaphragm sits much higher in the thoracic cavity than most singers realize. The top of the dome of the diaphragm sits at about the center of the breast. Most of the activity that a singer feels in the core of the body, which many singers and voice teachers mistake for diaphragmatic activity, is, in fact, engagement of the abdominal musculature. Exhalation used in everyday breathing is a passive process. Singing transforms exhalation from a passive process to an active one. Appelman describes the process below:

"The muscles of exhalation force the abdominal viscera inward and upward against the abdominal diaphragm, which is completely relaxed during exhalation. The volume of air within the lungs is forced outward in a steady, even breath stream as the dome of the diaphragm is thrust into the thoracic cavity and the walls of the thorax are forced inward by the action of the obliques and transverse and the depressor muscles of inspiration" (1967, 40).

Let's look closer at the major abdominal muscles of exhalation. We have three major sets of muscles in the abdomen. The most external layer of muscle is the rectus abdominis. The rectus abdominis is the large muscle that runs in sheaths vertically up the front of the body from the pubic bone and inserts into the base of the sternum and the fifth, sixth and seventh ribs of the ribcage. It is one of the strongest muscles in the body. Its action is to compress the abdominal viscera, forcing the contents inward. If you have ever done an abdominal crunch in the gym, you have contracted this muscle as you tried to

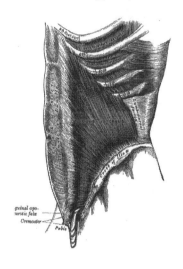

get your head to your knees. When toned, the rectus creates the coveted six-pack look that many men and women strive for.

We also have a set of abdominal muscles that run along the sides of the abdomen called the obliquus abdominis (the oblique muscles). You have certainly felt these muscles engage while exercising. The oblique muscles can be felt when you bring your left elbow to your right knee, rotating the body, or the right elbow to the left knee while twisting in the opposite direction. You have also felt these muscles engage when coughing. The obliques are divided into the internal obliques and the external obliques.

The internal obliques originate from the pelvis and top of the hip joint and the sides of the waist (lumbar fascia). The muscle fibers extend upward, crossing in an opposite direction from the fibers of the external obliques. They insert into the lower six costal cartilages of the ribs, into the rectus muscle and into an abdominal aponeurosis in the center of the abdomen. Their job is to depress the thorax and diminish the capacity of the abdomen.

The external oblique muscles originate from the exterior surfaces and lower borders of the eight inferior ribs. The oblique muscle fibers from the lower ribs course nearly vertically downward, inserting into the front of the top of the hip (the iliac crest). The oblique fibers from the middle and upper ribs course downward and forward, inserting into an abdominal aponeurosis in the center of the body. The external obliques also depress the thorax and compress the abdomen. The oblique muscle fibers form a long wide wall that greatly aids in controlling the breath during expiration.

The transversus abdominis muscle (transverse abdominal muscle) is the deepest of the abdominal muscles and is a major muscle of exhalation. It is a deep corset of muscle fibers below the rectus and obliques that run horizontally all the way across the front of the body. It courses from the inner surfaces of ribs 7 through 12, from the lumbar fascia at the sides of the waist and from the front of the hips (iliac crest) inserting into the centerline of the abdomen, all the way from the xiphoid process at the base of the sternum to the crest of the pubis. The transverse abdominal muscle has muscle fibers like fingers that rise from the top of the hips and connect with the diaphragm and costal muscles, making it an important muscle in exhalation. You can easily engage these muscle fibers if you try to draw your waist inward as if trying to make yourself skinnier. Notice that when you draw your waist inward, the circumference of the body gets smaller and the ribcage lifts upward all the way around. The transverse abdominal muscle is a deep muscle that most of us have little sensation of until we become involved in voice work. An awareness of the use of the abdominal muscles is very important to the singer and speaker. They regulate the pressure of the breath against the vocal cords and need to be finely mastered to create the perfect airstream to vocalize on.

BACK MUSCLES OF SUPPORT

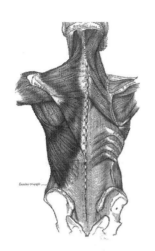

Since the thoracic ribcage is elevated and engaged in singing, some of the muscles of the back are working to assist the singer to delay exhalation. Two muscles worth describing are the lattissimus dorsi and the quadratus lumborum muscles.

A pair of muscles that must be included in the muscles of support are in our back and are called the latissimus dorsi. The muscle fibers of the latissimus dorsi originate from the lower half of the vertebral column of the spine, the last three or four ribs in the back of the ribcage and the top of the hip bone (iliac crest) by means of thoracic-lumbar fascia. They insert into the humerus (upper arm bone) in the shoulder joint. The latissimus dorsi contain muscle fibers that are able to elevate the ribs in the back of the ribcage, facilitating inspiration. The muscles contract during forced expiration, compressing the lower thorax and assisting in expiration. Voice scientists have found that during long periods of singing, muscular fatigue occurs in the lumbar-thoracic region, specifically in the latissimus dorsi. According to voice scientist D. Ralph Appelman, the latissimus dorsi, together with the abdominal muscles, create a sphincter that controls expiration (1967, 12). The quadratus lumborum is a paired, thick flat muscle located in the back of the abdomen that has also been described to act as a girdle around the lower back, directing the abdominal viscera upward towards the diaphragm when the abdominal muscles engage. It originates from the iliac crest and inserts into the lowermost rib and transverse processes of the lumbar vertebrae. It stabilizes the base of the thorax against the downward pull of the diaphragm. The science is not conclusive on either of these muscles.

BOAT POSE, *PARIPURNA NAVASANA*

Singers and actors need strong abdominal muscles. The contraction of the abdominal muscles, at the onset of tone, compresses the abdominal viscera upward and exerts a force against the diaphragm. When the abdominal muscles exert this force, the diaphragm engages. There is also a force directed toward the ribcage, which assists in lifting and supporting it. Without the engagement of the abdominal muscles, the ribcage will collapse and the body will rush to exhalation. The yoga posture boat pose is a great posture for strengthening the abdominal muscles. Sit down on the floor with your legs outstretched. Make sure you are sitting firmly on your sitting bones, the two bony points at the very base of the pelvis. Keep your chest up, the shoulders relaxed, the collarbones spread wide and the lower back drawn inward to create a neutral position for the spine. Bend your legs and slide your feet toward you until they rest on the ground a few feet in front of your hips. Reach your hands around the outside of the legs and grab the backs of the thighs. Lift the feet off the ground and stretch out the legs into the air. Let go of the legs and reach the hands forward with the palms facing each other, arms parallel to the ground. Now relax the belly, inhale and do lip buzzes on any pitch or scale. Feel the engagement in the epigastric area of the abdomen. If this posture is too hard, you can also do it with your hands on the back of the thighs, or on the floor behind you.

PANTING TO FEEL DIAPHRAGM

It is very difficult to actually feel the diaphragm, but we can feel its effect on other muscles in the torso. This exercise helps the student feel the abdominal support in the epigastric (space between the bottom of the breastbone and the navel) and umbilical (navel) regions of the torso. Find the spot at the bottom of the breastbone where the ribcage forms an upside down V. Put your fingers on this place. Stick your tongue out of your mouth and pant like a puppy. You will feel the action of the diaphragm on the abdominal musculature. As it lowers and rises, it presses against the viscera of the abdomen, making your belly move forward. By hanging the tongue out of the mouth, the air is not obstructed during the inflow or outflow of breath.

BREATH OF FIRE YOGA BREATHING

Kapalabhati pranayama breathing is extremely beneficial for cleansing the respiratory system of stale air and toxins. It is also a wonderful exercise to make the singer or speaker aware of how the abdominal muscles contribute to exhalation. Put your hand on your abdomen. Inhale through your nose into your belly and exhale quickly by pulling your abdomen in. Repeat rapidly, concentrating on the inward thrust of the belly, forcing exhalation. One of the major roles of the abdominal muscles is to force exhalation. You will notice that inhalation may naturally occur after such a strongly stimulated exhalation. Notice that the breath may reflexively drop back into your belly after exhalation when you relax it. Also, notice how quiet the inhalation is. There is no gasping or audible sound. The bodies of singers, chanters and actors can eventually become trained to let the breath quickly drop back in after the abdominal muscles have actively controlled the exhalation of sound. This is the reason that well-trained singers can often look as if they are not breathing at all.

Students always ask if they should relax or tense their abdomens on inhalation. You must relax your abdomen on inhalation, which is not always easy, because many of us have the habit of holding our bellies in to appear slimmer. So, hold your belly in and try to do "breath of fire" breathing. You will notice that your breath will not drop into your core and it is hard to engage the abdominal support. You will most likely feel tension in your throat and chest area. What feels better for breathing, a released abdomen or a tense one? Which way works better? Most voice teachers agree that a relaxed abdomen allows the body to inhale and exhale more freely.

PILATES BREATHING

 Joseph Pilates, the creator of the popular exercise system, Pilates, felt that learning to breathe was integral to doing his exercises correctly. The main focus of Pilates' training is to strengthen the core of a person, especially the deepest abdominal layer, the transverse abdominal muscle. Joseph Pilates required his clients to rib-swing breathe, letting the ribcage open and, when exhaling, to purse the lips and strongly exhale air, thus contracting and strengthening the core (Urla, 2008). The ribcage that opened on inhalation closed on exhalation. Today, many Pilates teachers have left out Joseph Pilates' important breathing techniques. The student is taught to strongly close the ribcage and maintain a closed ribcage position, even during breathing. This is problematic for singers and actors. Continuous, strong closing of the ribcage can overdevelop the intercostal (rib) muscles in a closed, exhalation position. A lack of flexibility in the ribcage can result, impeding good respiration.

BLOW OUT SIX CANDLES

This exercise is another very old singing exercise originating from the Italian School of Singing. It is fun to do this exercise lying on your back or standing. Imagine you are blowing out candles on a cake using the consonant ffff. Press your top teeth to your bottom lip to make an [f]. Notice how the abdominal muscles contract in the center of the torso, most notably between the base of the breastbone and the navel. Blow ffff, breathe and blow ffff, breathe and blow ffff. Keep going to six times.

OTHER HELPFUL CONSONANTS

There are other consonants aside from [f] that I call "hook-up" consonants. Hook-up consonants help the voice connect to its abdominal support. These consonants obstruct the breath stream in some way as it is leaving the mouth, enabling the speaker or singer to feel the support muscles in the core contract. Clear consonant articulation actually aids in good breath management.

> *Most of the activity that a singer feels in the core of the body, which many singers and voice teachers mistake for diaphragmatic activity, is, in fact, engagement of the abdominal musculature.*

The Italian School of Singing sometimes used unvoiced consonant exercises to increase the student's awareness of the abdominal support musculature of the voice (Miller, 1986, 33). Try sounding these unvoiced consonants first while lying on your belly and then on all fours.

An unvoiced consonant is a consonant that is made only using breath, so make sure that you are not using your vocal cords to add tone to the sound. Keep the throat relaxed and notice what happens in the core of your body when you articulate these consonants. Notice how your abdominal muscles are affected as you make each consonant. Do they move inward or outward? When lying down or on all fours, when you inhale, your belly should release downward and fill with air. When you articulate the consonant, your belly should move inward. The stronger you articulate the consonant, the stronger you will feel its reaction in the belly.

Unvoiced Consonants

P   as in Paul
T   as in Tom
S   as in Sam
TH as in Theatre
SH as in Shadow
CH as in Chin
K   as in Kangaroo

Now we are going to play with going from an unvoiced (breath only) consonant sound to a voiced (with tone) consonant sound. Each unvoiced consonant has a "partner" voiced consonant that is made by using the same method of articulation and mouth shape. For example: if you pucker your lips, you can make a [p] sound. If you keep the same puckered lips, you can also make a [b] sound, but the [b] sound has tone whereas the [p] sound was unvoiced.

Sound the following consonants while lying on your belly and on all fours again. See if these voiced consonants can have the same sensation in your abdomen as the unvoiced consonants. Don't let the consonants disconnect from your core just because they have tone. Stay out of your throat. Don't let the voiced consonants hit your vocal cords together during the onset of sound. Allow these voiced consonants to come from a deeper place in your body; let them have the sensation of starting in your abdomen. Remember, your throat is just to be used as a hallway to flow the air and sound through. You do not want to have the sensation of sound starting in your throat; then it is disconnected from its breath support. If you are having trouble with a consonant getting stuck in the throat, go back to using the corresponding unvoiced consonant sound until you feel its connection to your core. Then, gradually add tone while trying to keep the throat relaxed.

Voiced Consonants

B	as in Boy
D	as in Dog
Z	as is Zebra
Th	as in The
G	as in Genre
J	as in Judge
G	as in Go
V	as in Very
Wh	as in What

Corresponding Consonant Chart

Unvoiced		Voiced	
F	as in fat	V	as in very
P	as in Paul	B	as in boy
T	as in Tom	D	as in doctor
S	as in Sam	Z	as in zebra
TH	as in thigh	TH	as in thy
SH	as in shadow	G	as in genre
CH	as in chin	J	as in judge
K	as in Kara	G	as in go

Consonant to Vowel

Now, use any of the consonants in the consonant chart above to move from a consonant sound to a vowel. Let each of the consonants hook to your core, then allow the tone to open up on the vowel while maintaining the engagement of the abdominal support musculature. Now extend the breath through the vowel and sing faaaa.

ffff ffff faaaaaaah   ffff ffff faaaaah   ffff ffff faaaaah

REPETITION EXERCISE

The following exercise is derived from a singing exercise developed by Barbara Honn, Cincinnati Conservatory of Music, with revisions suggested by Ruth Falcon, Mannes School of Music. It is one of my favorite exercises to find the connection of the voice to the abdominal support musculature, and to see the close relationship between singing and speech. This exercise is very easy to remember and can result in marked improvement in a student's ability to connect the voice to the core.

If we speak without vocal sound, just using a whispered breath, the breath will naturally engage the abdominal support muscles of the voice in your core. So, in the first part of this exercise the student uses just breath to whisper the phrase.

Using just breath, say the following phrase two times:

> Re-pe-ti-tion, re-pe-ti-tion
> sh sh sh sh
> s s s s
> Fu-weet, fu-weet
> Fu-way, fu-way
> Fu-wah, fu-wah

Now, slowly transition from breath to actually speaking the phrase. Say the first word whispered and slowly move to actually voicing the word "repetition," keeping the same amount of muscle engagement in the core. Then, instead of saying the unvoiced [sh] consonant, replace it with a voiced French [j] (as in je suis) and replace the [s] consonant with a voiced [z] consonant. At the end, say two voiced "fu-weets."

Spoken:	Re-pe-ti-tion, re-pe-ti-tion
Voiced:	j, j, j, j (je suis)
Voiced:	z, z, z, z
Spoken:	Fu-weet, fu-weet
	Fu-way, fu-way
	Fu-wah, fu-wah

The third time you do the exercise, go from a breath "repetition" to a spoken "repetition" to a sung "repetition." You will notice that the sung "repetition" feels almost the same as the spoken version. End with a sung "vu-weet," instead of a "fu-weet."

Singing is a direct extension of speaking. In singing, the vowels are lengthened and more air moves through the phrase, but the sensation of the voice connected to the core of the body should be the same.

Sung:	Re-pe-ti-tion, re-pe-ti-tion
Sung:	j, j, j, j (je suis)
Sung:	z, z, z, z
Sung:	Vu-weet, vu-weet

Most students notice that the word "vu-weet" will cause the following experience: the "vu" articulated by putting the top teeth on the bottom lip will cause the abdominals to engage and the "wee" will cause the abdominals to quickly pop inward, resulting in a higher pitched sound. The "fuweet" or "vuweet" word is excellent to use for practicing big ascending leaps in music. It identifies the abdominal energy required in the core to move the voice up to a higher pitch.

STRAW EXERCISE

This is a favorite exercise of noted voice scientist Ingo Titze at the National Center for Voice and Speech in Salt Lake City, Utah. If you are having trouble finding the sensation of abdominal activation in your core, do this exercise. Take a plastic drinking straw and put it in your mouth. Hum a tone into the straw. Hum up and down the scale and notice how easily you can feel your abdominal muscles contracting. As you go higher up the scale, you will feel more of your abdominal muscles contract as they work harder to support higher pitches.

BARKING EXERCISE

Students sometimes mention that when their dogs bark, they see their bellies move in and out, and it seems as if their voices are coming from the sides of their body. This exercise is a barking exercise. You will feel silly doing it, but it is very effective. Get on your hands and knees, relax your belly and let your belly hang to the floor. Make some barking "woof woof" sounds, feeling the belly gently move upward on each "woof." Try to connect the bark to the abdominal musculature in your belly and stay out of the throat area. If you feel the vocal cords hitting together, stay on the [w] longer and be sure to end on the [f]. Try to make a sound with full tone, as opposed to a breathy tone. Also, try not to move your back. The latissimus dorsi muscles may engage in barking so you may want to move your back, but don't. Try to isolate what the muscles in your belly are doing when you bark. See what muscles naturally engage and what way they move. The belly should move upward when you bark. Now try being a singing dog and sing "woof" up and down the scale.

LIP BUZZES

This is a fantastic old singing exercise for gaining the awareness of the feeling of the activation of the abdominal musculature and the intercostals (rib muscles), and a favorite exercise of singers. Take a breath and buzz your lips on any pitch. Put your hand on the space between the navel and the base of the breastbone (the epigastrium). You will feel the abdominal support musculature of the voice engage when you buzz. Notice that your abdomen moves outward when you inhale, remains stationary in a state of suspension and then gently moves inward the longer you go on your breath stream.

To engage lip buzzing using your abdominal muscles, inhale expanding the base of the ribcage and the abdomen and then gently tap your abdomen inward. Most find that it is best to tap inward between the base of the breastbone and navel, or around the navel area. The activation of the abdominal musculature naturally helps the ribcage stay lifted. Do not squeeze the ribcage inward to induce buzzing. The ribcage should stay expanded. The whole sheath of abdominal muscles will engage. They will suspend for a time, not moving inward or outward, and the epigastric area may bulge slightly outward in response to the diaphragm and abdominal muscles pressing against each other. When you are running out of air the lower abdominal area below the epigastrium will slowly move inward. The action of the abdominal muscles and ribcage in this exercise most closely resembles what we want in breath management for singing and is also a great exercise to begin to experience *appoggio*. Therefore, it is great training for the body.

Many people have difficulty getting their lips to buzz. The first thing you will notice is that your lips will not buzz if you do not start with enough energy, and the energy comes by tapping the abdominal muscles inward. Lip buzzes show that singing is much more athletic than everyday speech; therefore, it requires more energy and vitality. Secondly, there is a direct correlation between the ribcage and the ability to buzz the lips. You will only be able to buzz your lips as long as you are able to control the descent of the ribcage and keep the intercostal muscles and abdominal musculature active. Do not squeeze the ribcage closed to try to get extra air out. Squeezing it inward will create tension in the throat and eliminate the breath too quickly. This is the opposite action for voice work. The ribcage should stay open and slowly float down, delaying exhalation. Keeping the abdominal muscles engaged helps delay the ribcage from closing. Practice buzzing your lips until you can buzz them for 20 seconds. All singers need to master this exercise as it closely mirrors what actually takes place in the vocal cords when singing. The vocal cords buzz, just like a pair of lips, in response to the airstream coming up the trachea. The air needs to be paced evenly at a steady pressure against the vocal cords to emit a stable tone.

R TRILLS

Some people cannot buzz their lips. In this case, you can use your tongue and sing on a rolled, Latin [r]: [rrrrrrrrrrrrrrrrrrrrrrrrrrrr]. Put the tip of your tongue to the roof of your mouth and see if you can create a Latin [r]. This is fun to do, even if you can buzz your lips. You will also feel the muscles activate in your core when rolling the [r]. This exercise is also fantastic for relaxing the tongue and is especially good for singers or actors who have a lot tension in the tongue. The tongue is a bundle of muscle fibers, and the vigorous action the tongue makes against the roof of the mouth while making the Latin [r] exercises the deepest layers of it.

SINGING INTO A WALL

Find a wall that you can lean on. Straighten your arms out shoulder height in front of you until your palms rest on the wall. Keeping your palms on the wall, put your feet 2 to 2½ feet away from the wall so that you can lean into the wall. Keep your body straight as a board and lean your weight against the wall as you sound on ahhhh. Try a Greek lament like *oy toi toi*. Try to lean into the wall from

the core of your body and become aware of the support muscles of the voice that engage as you sound. When doing this exercise, most people find that they can sustain a loud tone for a long time and can go longer on the breath than usual. Try singing a difficult passage this way. This exercise is especially good for male singers who have to increase their energy and support as they go higher in their register. It is also terrific for modern styles of singing like belting.

BACK TO THE WALL

Put your back against a wall. Now slide your back down the wall until your knees are bent and it looks like you are sitting in an imaginary chair. Press your back into the wall, take a breath and sound on a loud ahhhh. The region you want to especially focus on pressing into the wall is the lower third of the ribcage and waist area. You will find that in this position, you can get very loud and go much longer on your breath than usual. Now try singing part of a song or reciting text that you are working on. You will notice a lot of muscle activation in the costal muscles and the latissimus dorsi muscles in the back. Also, the abdominal muscles in the core will engage. Notice how the latissimus dorsi back muscles engage and how they contribute to support singing. This exercise and the previous exercise make the singer aware of the vitality and muscular energy required in the core for singing.

SINGING VINYASA SERIES

I have always enjoyed vocalizing while doing my yoga practice. Joan Melton, in her book *One Voice, Integrating Singing Technique and Theatre Voice Training* (2000), has found that rounded body positions are better for sounding high notes and arched body positions are better for low notes (2000, 82). Singing while doing a *vinyasa* yoga flow series assists the voice in releasing freely from the body in its natural, authentic form. Don't withhold the voice or try to overcontrol the voice when doing

these exercises. Also, do not push the voice. Pushing will only cause tension in the throat and result in a tighter, squeezed sound. Let the sound of the voice flow out freely in whatever primal way it chooses. Remember, your voice is breath so make sure that you have a feeling of the voice riding out on the breath from the core of the body. Once the voice is free, you can later refine it with Bel Canto singing techniques.

Start standing with your palms together at your chest in prayer pose. Float your arms down to your sides and inhale as you lift your arms overhead to meet, palm to palm. Exhale while singing a descending scale (a high to low series of tones) on "ah," as you bring your arms out parallel to the floor and bend over toward your feet. Singing will be the exhalation as the voice rides out on the breath. Don't be too concerned with hitting specific pitches. It is more important to get the voice moving. This descending scale should feel as easy as a sigh.

Breathe into the lower back and put your hands on your shins, rising up halfway. Fold back over toward the ground while singing a descending scale on "ah" again. While hanging over, see if you can feel the lower back expand with breath. Breathe all the way down to the base of the spine and sing a low note, imagining the tone starting from the base of the spine. Sing an ascending, sliding scale (from a low pitch to a high pitch) on "ah." As you sing higher up the scale, feel the sound move up the spine and end in the head. Relax the jaw and try hanging your tongue out of the mouth as you sing "ah." You can even wiggle the tongue against the top teeth to make sure it relaxes and does not engage during your voiced exhalation.

Inhale and come down into plank (push up position). Relax the belly around the navel. Breathe, feeling the breath come into the belly, and see if you can feel the vibration of the voice activating in the same place. The core of the body is very engaged in plank, and it can be hard to breathe, so keep releasing and inhaling into the belly. Stay in plank and try singing short, speech-level or low tones on a "huh." See if you can feel the tones originating from the belly. If you feel any tension in your throat, change the "huh" to "fuh." High tones don't feel as natural in this posture and they may cause tightening in the throat, so stick to low, primal tones.

Inhale and come down into upward dog or cobra. Cobra is easier on your lower back. While in upward dog or cobra, breathe and make sure you feel the breath expanding the whole front of the torso on inhalation. It can be difficult to hold long notes in cobra or upward dog, so sing short, speech-level or low tones on "huh" or "fuh." See if you can feel the abdominal muscles engage as you make sound. Try singing a series of rapid staccato (separated) notes on "huh." This is a great posture for working on your lower register.

Inhale into the belly and come into downward dog. This posture is amazing to expand the breath capacity of the singer, so try breathing in a variety of ways before singing in this posture. While in downward dog, the core is once again very active, so consciously release the belly around the navel and breathe into it. Now try breathing into the sides of the torso. See if you can feel the sides of the waist expanding outward. It may feel as if the bottom ribs and the top of your hip bones are moving outward. Now try breathing just into the middle back, expanding the lower portion of the ribcage. Begin expanding the ribcage at its base and see, as you add more air, if you can expand more and more of the back all the way up to the shoulder blades. It may feel as if your back is arching up into a hump as the ribs open up. By opening up the back, the lungs are stretched in areas that are usually not active. The more flexibility and mobility in the ribcage, the more the lungs can expand and increase lung power.

Downward dog is comfortable to sing in. You will find that the middle and upper registers of your voice are easy to get into. Sing some high notes on "woo." Try sliding the voice up and down the scale and see if you can once again feel the voice coming from the base of the spine, traveling up the spine and ending in the head on the highest notes. High tones will create a lot of pressure in the head in downward dog, but it shows the singer where head tones or falsetto notes need to resonate.

Practice singing a song in downward dog. Feel the voice riding out on the breath unobstructed by tension. If you are feeling any tension while singing, make sure your jaw and tongue are relaxed. Shake your head to make sure the skull is loose. It is fun to stick the tongue out of the mouth and let it hang toward the ground as you sound in downward dog.

Inhale and walk your hands back to your feet. Continue to hang over and breathe. Warm down the voice with some easy "oo's." Then inhale and slowly raise your arms upward as you come back to standing, touching your palms together overhead. End the sequence by singing an "om" on any pitches you choose as you bring your palms back to prayer pose. Your voice and body should feel warmed up for singing.

CAT AND DOG

This is a great exercise to become aware of how the abdominal muscles assist in exhalation.

Get on your hands and knees. Inhale and arch your back into dog posture as you look up. Remain in this position and release your abdominal muscles, feeling your belly hang toward the ground. Inhale and exhale a few times. Notice that the belly will move outward on inhalation and inward on exhalation. Inhale into the belly and exhale very slowly on an "shhhh." The breath should engage the abdominal muscles. Follow the pace of the exhalation as your abdominals move little by little toward the spine on "shhhh," and arch up into cat posture. Inhale back into dog posture and repeat. Let the length of the breath control the timing of the movement of the body into a fully arched cat posture. Try the exercise on a French [j] as in *je suis*. See if you can feel the vibration of tone in your belly as you do this exercise with sound.

According to voice scientist Ralph Appelman, the latissimus dorsi, together with the abdominal muscles, create a sphincter that controls expiration.

For singing we need to increase the vertical space between our top and bottom teeth in the back of our mouth, as many of us actually speak with our teeth closed.

Chapter Six

APPOGGIO AND THE LOTTA VOCALE

SINGING AND SPEECH ARE DIFFERENT

YOU HAVE PROBABLY HEARD THAT we sing and speak with the same voice. There are many teachers who base their complete singing technique on speech-based singing. An old adage from the Italian School of Singing is *si canta comme si parla*, which means, sing as you speak. The singing voice should be a direct extension of the speaking voice, but there are two main differences between singing and speaking, and the clue is in the word extension. Singing is extending the speaking voice. Richard Miller says in his book, *Solutions for Singers*, that singing requires a higher rate of breath energy and an elongation of the breath cycle (2004, 18). Speech uses short bursts of air and singing uses a slow controlled stream of air. To achieve the elongation of the breath cycle for singing, *appoggio* is the technique most widely recognized as the best.

Si canta comme si parla is limited to the speech-inflection range of the voice. A singing teacher will often begin voice training using the pitches that the student naturally speaks on. As the singer sings higher up the scale, speech-like production is not adequate and there may be a need for certain physiological and acoustic modifications. According to Richard Miller, breath management, duration of vowels, range, energy and technical requirements of the singing voice far exceed that of speech (1996, 52).

APPOGGIO AND THE LOTTA VOCALE

The very first schools of singing began in Italy and were created to prepare choirs to sing the liturgical chants of the Roman Catholic Church. The earliest known school of singing for chant was founded in the fourth century by Pope Sylvester (314-336 AD). The employment of trained singers in the service of the church in its earliest centuries led to the institution, in 590 AD, of the famous *Schola Cantorum* of Pope Gregory (540-604 AD). As early as 535 AD, there is evidence of manuals of instruction used by teachers of chant, but the earliest manuals that survived intact are from the sixteenth century.

The first national schools of singing emerged in the seventeenth century. Different schools developed in different areas and different breath control techniques emerged from each of them. The German School was famous for what it called *Bauchaussenstüze*, which required the singer to inhale into the abdomen and push out on the belly while singing. The English School of Singing required the singer to pull in the abdomen, while singing, which created the straight-toned voices of English choirs due to a higher breath pressure system. The Italian School of Singing has been the most favored resource for breath management techniques in singing. The Italian School named their form of breath management *appoggio*. *Appoggio* can be described as the inhalation muscles leaning against the exhalation muscles. The goal in the Italian School was to create, with the use of *appoggio*, the *lotta vocale*, (in Italian) or *lutte vocale* (in French), the vocal struggle or vocal contest.

Francesco Lamperti (1813-1892) and his son Giovanni Battista Lamperti (1839-1910) were two of the most famous voice teachers of all time. The elder Lamperti felt that the best way to achieve breath control was through the use of *appoggio*. He wrote that "by singing *appoggiata* is meant that all notes, from the highest to the lowest, are produced over a column of air by which the singer has perfect command, by holding back the breath" (1890, 18). How to clearly achieve *appoggio* was first explained in 1876, when a famous physiologist in Paris, Dr. Louis Mandl (1812-1881), wrote a treatise on the voice, *Hygiéne de la Voix*, that revolutionized the world of singing. Mandl stated that the "*lutte vocale (lotta vocale)* is primarily the struggle between the abdominal muscles and the diaphragm, and that this struggle is reflected in the contractions of the larynx as well" (Stark, 2003, 100). Francesco Lamperti was an admirer of Mandl and introduced his theory of the *lotta vocale* in his book *The Art of Singing* (1890). Lamperti's description of the *lotta vocale* is still widely used by singing teachers today (1890, 21):

"To sustain a given note, the air should be expelled slowly; to attain this end, the respiratory (inspiratory) muscles, by continuing their action, strive to retain air in the lungs, and oppose their action to that of the expiratory muscles, which is called *lutte vocale*, or vocal struggle. On the retention of this equilibrium depends the just emission of the voice, and by which means of it alone can true expression be given to the sound produced."

Lamperti's Appoggio Exercise

Francesco Lamperti's (1813-1892) original *appoggio* breathing exercise greatly expanded the ribcage and required the singer to have complete control over the ribcage. He said that this exercise would give the singer the sensation of the *lotta vocale* (1928, 17).

"*Appoggio* is produced by holding back the breath. The singer should take eighteen seconds to fill the lungs completely with air. Then the singer should slowly emit a stream of breath, taking eighteen seconds for its expulsion, holding back the breath as much as possible."

Get a clock with a second hand and try this exercise. As you inhale, only sip in a tiny bit of air so you don't crowd the lungs too soon. You will notice that eighteen seconds is a very long time to inhale. As you slowly release air on the exhalation, it is normal to feel a great deal of pressure within the costal muscles of the ribs. Also, there will be a tendency for the breath to want to rush out to induce a new breath.

Richard Miller, in his numerous books on singing, advocates the use of *appoggio* and describes the physical sensations quite well. He says that the breath is quietly taken in, either through the mouth or the nose, the epigastric and umbilical regions move outward and the base of the ribs and flanks open laterally. There is a slight lift in the pectoral region as the sternum lifts in response to the opening of the ribcage, but the lungs are never overcrowded and the shoulders remain relaxed, never being used to lift the ribcage. Miller says that we do not want the epigastric and umbilical regions to move in too soon, in order to create a dynamic equilibrium on which we can regulate the expulsion of breath (2004, 2). This equilibrium is a sort of state of suspension that a singer wants to feel, where the ribcage stays lifted and the abdominals are not pushed out or pulled in but remain active without rigidity. The lungs can expel the air at an even pace because the exhalation muscles have not taken over. At a certain point on the breath stream, the exhalation muscles do become stronger than the inhalation muscles, the abdominals move inward and the ribcage starts to slowly float down. However, once again, we want this to happen without tension and rigidity and especially without squeezing the ribs upon closure.

Most singers find that *appoggio* is similar to the feeling in the muscles of the ribs and in the abdominals that is felt when you buzz your lips. Lip buzzes are a fantastic exercise to develop *appoggio* technique.

Mastering *appoggio* and achieving the *lotta vocale* takes considerable time and training. Many beginning singers have little sensation of their interior musculature and little mastery over these muscles. It takes time and training to bring the body fully under the singer's control; but don't despair, all of the exercises in this book will lead you there.

CREATING APPOGGIO

The major element of *appoggio* is learning to maintain the *appoggio* posture. The *appoggio* posture is a lifted sternum position with an expanded ribcage sometimes called the "noble posture."

How do you do this? Relax the abdomen and take a deep breath, allowing the bottom third of the ribcage and your waist to expand outward all the way around your body. Let the sternum lift as the ribcage expands on inhalation. Once lifted, do not allow the sternum to drop and do not allow the ribcage to recoil on exhalation. Remember, there is a direct correlation between a lifted sternum and the openness of the ribcage. If you hold the sternum up, the ribcage will stay open. Some teachers teach you to muscularly lift the sternum before inhalation, but I find that this can lead to tension in the neck and shoulders. You can naturally find this position if your ribcage lifts on inhalation. If not, practice the belly dance ribcage lift exercise. You can also hold your arms behind your back to facilitate practicing the posture.

HE HE EXERCISE

The well-known voice teacher and author Richard Miller did 20 minutes of these exercises every morning, and he swore that they kept him singing into his seventies (2004, 32). This exercise is a very old exercise from the Italian School of Singing. Some teachers have called it a pulse exercise. You will sing on the vowel [e] like the [e] in "hello." This exercise will expose the tendency of the student to initiate sound first in the vocal cords (especially on vowels) and give the student an opportunity to get the sound to originate from a deeper place in the core of the body. The tendency at first is to try to sound the [e] in the throat and hit the cords together, adding a little [h] sound as if you were saying hey, or to make a glottal stroke, which is a little grunt made with the vocal cords at the onset of the vowel sound. See if you can get the [e] to first engage the abdominal support muscles in the core. Relax your abdominal muscles and breathe expanding the bottom of the ribcage and waist area. Imagine you are singing down a long tube as if you were a clarinet, with the bottom of the clarinet at the navel. Since you want to begin with breath first, see if you can get the sound to move your epigastric area (the space between the bottom of the breastbone and the navel). Once you feel the abdomen engage, see if you can sing the exercises staying connected to the abdominal musculature, but with minimal movement in the epigastrium. If you are feeling your vocal cords hitting together first, then do this exercise starting with an [m], humming on the [m] and then go to the [e]. If you are still starting the sound at the vocal cords, then do this exercise using "mo oh oh." The rounder "oh" sound is easier for many singers to feel deeper within the body, but eventually you want to be able to do this exercise with the more difficult [e] sound.

Breathe and sing an [e] [e], breathe and repeat.

Then add three [e] [e] [e], breathe and repeat.

Then four [e] [e] [e] [e], breathe and repeat.

Then try five and six staccato sounds with a catch breath between each group.

FIVE EXERCISE

My version of the Richard Miller exercise uses the word five. Put your hand on the epigastric region. Remember that this is the space below the bottom of the breastbone and above the navel. Sing or speak on one pitch the word five, sounding on the vowel. Feel the engagement of the abdominal musculature beneath your hand. You will notice that the musculature bounces or pulses. Try to minimize the movement while still keeping the engagement. Try to get the sound to feel as if it originates in your core not in your throat. Make sure to use your top teeth against your bottom lip to clearly articulate the [f].

Fa, ha, ha, ha, ive (breathe) repeat.
Fa, ha, ha, ha, ha, ive (breathe) repeat.
Fa, ha, ha, ha, ha, ha, ive (breathe) repeat.

Once you have mastered the staccato (bouncy) exercises above, you will try some legato (smooth) exercises.

Sing the word five and sing up the major scale. If you don't know the major scale, sing any series of ascending notes.

Fa-ah-ah-ah-ah-ah-ah-ive (do re mi fa so la ti do).

*While standing still, a singer needs a
silent current of energy coursing through
his or her body to excite the breath
stream and energize the voice.*

Chapter Seven

SINGING, TRANSFORMING ENERGY

SINGING IS A FEAT OF TRANSFORMING ENERGY

WHAT WE EXPECT OF SINGERS is quite remarkable. We expect them to stand in one place and, with a sense of grace and ease, emit beautiful sounds full of energy and emotion, to transform us to another place. This is much harder to do than one might expect. Beginning singers will have a tendency to try to sing with the same energy that they use for speech. This will not work. The resulting sound will usually be an out-of-tune, devitalized sound that does not contain what we call "the singer's formant" (frequencies that create a beautiful ring in the voice). Singing is very athletic and requires much more energy than everyday speech. Athletes know that they need to energize their bodies before competitions so they often jump around to get energized for athletic performance. Singers have to do the same thing; they are vocal athletes and need to put on a state of physical readiness for performance. The energy required for singing sometimes more closely resembles what a beginning singer might use for yelling, and in the case of belting, singing is actually beautified yelling. A fun exercise to do is to jog in place and sing. Usually the voice will come out stronger, and as you sing higher up the scale, the energy of jogging will actually help you hit the higher notes. Voice teachers can get a more accurate idea of a student's vocal range by having the student sing from the lowest note possible to his or her highest note while jogging. Most people will be able to sing higher up the scale, as the heightened energy in jogging gives them the breath energy to hit the notes. But, we can't always sing and jog, so singers have to be able to create energy in their bodies, even when they are standing still. They have to be able to create an inner electricity that I call "a silent current of energy," to excite the breath from the core of the body, so that the voice has energy to propel it into motion. An adage in an old Italian singing treatise said that nervous people make better singers. I thought this was a rather odd statement, but then I pondered the thought and realized that nervous people usually have a lot of extra energy coursing through their veins, which could very likely be harnessed to energize the voice. To put on a state of energetic, physical readiness, I sometimes instruct my students, especially when singing a high piece of music, to imagine that they have just drunk a double espresso. They need to manifest an inner electrical current to energize their voice. I also have students gently bounce on their feet to create energy. Bouncing gives them the energy to spin their notes higher, easier.

Singing with emotion can also give singers energy to propel the voice. The other day I was driving to a summer outdoor performance and I was having some allergies. I got to the gig and noticed that we were playing on a green lawn in an outside venue by the beach. There was a lot of wind, green grass and pollen flying about that was dreadful for singing. The first set went fine, but I felt like I was missing that special magic, and my voice just didn't have the power and clarity that I like it to have. At the beginning of the second set, I decided to really get into the emotion of a blues song. All of sudden I felt a churning of energy in the center of my core and my breath had more spin to it. Finally, my voice felt alive. Then an old adage from the Bel Canto School of Singing popped into my head: "Sing with emotion and it will help the voice." Creating energy for the voice requires some sort of catalyst; we can't always jump up and down (which would work), so a more subtle, but powerful way is to use our emotions. Passion creates energy to excite the voice, which will also transfer to the audience.

LARGE INTERVAL LEAPS IN MUSIC

Not only do singers have to be able to create energy to power the voice, but also different parts of our voice require different amounts of energy. Sing a low note just below speaking. You will notice that you will not need to make an energy shift in your body. Sing a note right around the pitches that you usually speak on. We are so used to the energy required for the middle range of our everyday speech that most of us will be able to sing a decent speaking range note without making any adjustments. Most untrained singer's voices will start to fall apart as they move up the scale, above speech. As the singer sings up the scale, he or she needs to increase the energy level of the body. Singers actually change energy in the silence between notes and are masters of making rapid energy shifts. The space between two notes is an active space; singers are doing things that may not be audible, but are still very important for the production of sound. As we sing up the scale, there is a need for a systematic change in energy levels. Each note up the scale, above the comfortable pitches we speak on, will require an increase in energy. Singers have to be able to instantly fabricate a silent current of energy without inducing any tension in the body. We previously discussed how the energy we induce is similar to the sort of energy you get when you are excited, or when you drink too many cappuccinos and feel hyperactive. If athletes are running a 5K race, they may pace themselves at first, not running as hard as they can, until another competitor comes close and threatens their chance at winning. At that point, the athlete will put on a burst of energy to jump ahead of the competitor. Singers have to do the same thing in the middle of a song when faced with big interval leaps. Higher notes in our singing registers will require higher levels of energy. One of the biggest interval jumps in singing, which we often see in songs, is the octave jump. An octave, from *oct*, meaning eight, is eight steps higher up the scale. Octave jumps are really just energy level jumps. A perfect example of a song that contains an octave jump requiring an increase in energy is *Happy Birthday*. Next time you are in a restaurant where someone is celebrating a birthday, listen to the waiters sing *Happy Birthday*. The beginning will usually be fine, *happy birthday to you, happy birthday to you*, but, the third line, *happy birthday*, requires an octave jump up the scale. Most of the waiters will not know how to increase the energy level, so they will sing the word, *birthday* flat, and it will not sound good. Trained singers, in the silence between the word *happy* and the octave jump upward, will activate energy in their bodies to excite their air to reach the higher note. The result will be a louder, more energized top note, resulting in the singer actually hitting the pitch.

Jogging Exercise

Sing while jogging in place. Let your breath be stimulated and sing up and down the scale. Notice if you can go any higher up the scale while jogging.

Jumping Exercise

Go through any song you are working on and notice any big leaps up the scale. These places in the song will require changes in energy, so mark these changes in your music. Now, sing the song and jump up in the air for every high note. Sing the song again while increasing your energy silently for the higher note without jumping.

Preparation Exercise

You can also prepare for a high note coming up in a song by energizing the previous notes. Sing the note before a high jump with much more energy than is necessary for the pitch. Now, try to gradually increase the energy on a phrase leading up to a big jump so that, when the large interval jump happens, you are already prepared. You will then have enough energy for the jump up in pitch.

When the air coming up the trachea hits the vocal cords, it excites them into vibration and is then transformed into sound-colored air.

Chapter Eight

SOUND-COLORED AIR AND AIRFLOW

THE VOICE IS SOUND-COLORED AIR

THE ITALIAN MASTERS SAID, "UPON the freedom of the breath is the freedom of the voice." The voice does not exist without the breath. The whole process of speaking or singing is an air voyage. Beginning singers often alter their method of exhalation once they add sound to their air, as if the voice were a separate entity from the breath. The voice and the breath are one and the same. A singer begins singing by inhaling and allowing air to enter the bottom of the lungs. Air then leaves the lungs, goes up the trachea and flows through the vocal cords. When the air hits the vocal cords, it excites them into vibration and is then transformed into tone, which I like to call sound-colored air. The tone then rides up into the resonators and out of the mouth. The air doesn't disappear at the vocal cords, when it turns into sound. The sound that you emit is still the same air from the lungs, but it has been transformed into sound waves. Singing is allowing the voice to take a sound journey without any part of the body interfering with the air movement. This is easy to say but not so easy to achieve. Any tension in the body will obstruct airflow, and beginning singers often have a difficult time letting their voice move freely. That means no clenching of any part of the throat, jaw, mouth cavity or tongue.

A big part of voice training is training the body to get used to increased air pressures as you attempt to expand your vocal range and play with increased volumes. Many singers have what we call "fear of heights," a fear of singing higher up the scale. At first, singers will often believe that they can't sing high and will psychologically hinder the ability to hit high notes. Most people have the ability to sing much higher than they realize. An important part of voice training is to show our bodies and our minds that we can go much further with our voice than we think, and that it is safe and fun to expand our vocal horizons.

Experienced singers often talk about letting the voice spin on the air. The Italians called this technique *filar il suono,* to spin out the sound (Coffin 1989, 99). When singers sing a good high note, they often say that there was a lot of spin in the note. Spinning air is a skill that singers need to practice just like any other skill required for singing, and the following exercises will give you a chance to explore this new technique.

Vroom Exercise

Touch your top teeth to your bottom lip and make a [v] sound. Don't sing a [v], but instead, see if you can make a [v] sound like an engine of some sort; a mechanical, breathy sound, as if you were mimicking the sound of a motorcycle revving its engine, "vroom-vroom." Your bottom lip may tickle. Little boys often like to mimic the sound of cars and motorcycles by doing this. The sound you make will not sound like singing, but instead, like some sort of mechanical whirring sound. My students often say that it sounds like an alien spaceship landing. Start on your lowest note and vroom up the scale, up to your highest note. By partial occlusion (closing) of the vocal tract, a very gentle favorable pressure is exerted on the vocal cords, allowing them to stretch in a very healthful way. This exercise also takes you through the register changes of the voice and helps smooth the transitions. One of the things I like best about this exercise is that it creates a spin in the air and gives the singer the sensation of what spinning the voice actually feels like. This is the best exercise to experience *filar il suono* (spin the sound). As a singer sings up the scale into the higher register, he or she will want the voice to flow freely without contracting any of the muscles in the throat. If the voice spins on the air, there is never any sensation of muscling the voice out of the body. Instead, the voice floats on the air and the singer experiences a sensation of releasing and freeing the voice.

Va Va Exercise

After doing the "vroom" exercise, try this exercise. Once you can vroom up and down the scale, start to separate your top teeth slightly from your bottom lip and sing a "va-va." Go back and forth between the "vroom" to the "va," still trying to keep the sensation of the air spinning. You will notice, as you go higher up the scale, that your top teeth can come farther away from your bottom lip to create more room for the voice to release. This is a great exercise to get your air moving and to get you to learn to sing on the release of air.

Sing Through Straws to Stretch Cords

This is another favorite exercise of voice scientist Ingo Titze. Get different sizes of drinking straws and hum up and down the scale through each straw. The straw extends the length of your vocal tract to the very end of the straw,

creating a smaller, longer, tubular instrument. The result is a gentle, low air pressure flow against your vocal cords, which allows them to stretch very safely. This exercise is also great for blending registers. Notice how easy it is to sing across register breaks in the voice while singing through the straw. Singing through straws can also help the student feel the sensation of abdominal support for the voice. Put your hand on your belly and, as you sing higher up the scale, notice the contraction of the abdominal muscles. Notice which pitches create more muscle activation in your abdomen.

Scary Story "Woooo"

Imagine you are telling some children a scary story about a night when the wind was blowing loudly. Imitate the sound of the wind by shaking your voice and saying "woooooooooooooo." Now sing this "woooo" all the way up and down the scale and see if you can get the voice to ride on the air, not allowing any of the vocal tract muscles to tighten. See if you can feel the air spinning. It actually helps to spin your hand around in a circle as you sound. Don't think you are singing. It is better to think you are just making crazy sounds, because, often when we begin to sing, we tense up.

Song on a Whisper

With whatever song you choose, sing the song on a whisper. Make sure you can feel the air emitting from your body throughout each phrase of the song.

Song on Shhhh

Sing a song on shhhh instead of a whisper and watch how the ribcage naturally paces its descent, to pace the exhalation of air.

Song on Zzzzz

Now sing the same song on a zzzzz and see if you can still keep the voice moving without tensing any part of your body now that you have added tone to the air.

Wows!

Start in a comfortable speaking pitch and glide your voice up the scale while you say, "Wow!" Open your mouth bigger as you get higher. As a singer sings higher up the scale, the singer always needs to open the mouth more. Don't think you are singing. Instead, imagine you have been surprised by something and have responded by letting out a big "Wow." When we use our voice spontaneously, with enthusiasm, we often release a loud, tension-free sound.

ENERGY CHANNELS, *NADIS*

Voice work is also energy work. When we move our breath and our voice, we move energy within our body. Singers often have the sensation of breath energy coursing from the bottom of their torso, up the spine and through the chakras.

The ancient traditions of yoga teach that there are indeed invisible energy channels within the body that course alongside and in the center of the spine. A wonderful result of voice work can be the opening of these channels. In yoga, these channels are called *nadis*. *Nadis* comes from the word *nad*, meaning a hollow stalk, resonance, sound and vibration. There are 350,000 *nadis* or energy channels in the body. The *nadis* in yoga correspond to the meridians of traditional Chinese medicine.

The three most important *nadis* are the *susumna*, the *ida* and the *pingala*. Up the center of the spine runs the *susumna nadi*. It begins at the root of the torso, runs through the center of the spine and ends in the thousand-petaled lotus crown chakra, *sahasrara*. On the left of the spine runs the *ida nadi* and on the right side of the spine courses the *pingala*. The *ida* and *pingala nadis* crisscross each other as they spiral upwards and connect to opposite nostrils. The *pingala nadi* is the carrier of active solar energy and is associated with the sympathetic nervous system. The *ida nadi* is the carrier of passive lunar energy and corresponds with the parasympathetic nervous system. The *ida* and *pingala* are thought to be active in all human beings, but the *susumna* is dormant, waiting to be awakened by the yoga practitioner. When a source of prana energy, called *kundalini*, is activated, the *ida* and *pingala* are thought to merge with the *susumna*.

Kundalini is prana energy that is dormant within all of us. It is represented by a coiled serpent lying asleep at the bottom of the trunk at the site of the *mudlahara* chakra. When the *kundalini* is awakened, the serpent uncoils and rises up the *susumna nadi,* activating all the chakras.

Spine Breathing

While standing or sitting with a straight spine, close your eyes and say zoh on the lowest note that you can, feeling the tone vibrate in your lower torso. See if you can feel the tone in the pelvic floor. Slide up the scale to your highest easy note, visualizing the tone vibrating up your spine, through the *ida* and *pingala nadis* into the head and out the top of your head. Now, imagine the *kundalini* serpent coiled three times at the base of your pelvic floor. Sing into the serpent and imagine it uncoiling and sending the vibration of sound and breath up the center of your spine, through the *susumna nadi* and out your crown chakra.

BREATHY PHONATION

When learning to sing, try to sing as loudly as you comfortably can. When speaking, also try to speak with a full, energized voice. If you sing or speak too lightly, there will not be enough energy for the breath to excite the cords into a complete closure, resulting in breathy phonation. Women are most guilty of this habit, as they often want to speak in a breathy, soft voice, thinking that devitalized vocal production is more feminine. Think of Jackie Kennedy or Marilyn Monroe, who both spoke in the breathy soft voices that were popular for women in their time. I still meet women who speak in soft, childish or breathy voices. Speaking or singing with a breathy tone actually requires the vocal cords to not completely close. They are held slightly apart, which results in a breathy sound.

If your voice is not usually breathy and suddenly changes, it could be a symptom of a vocal problem. The sudden onset of a breathy voice, or a scratchy or gravely voice, may be the result of serious problems with your vocal cords or your health. If you have had a normal sounding voice and your voice changes, it is important to see a doctor as soon as possible.

Normally, we do not want to use a breathy voice, but breathy phonation is a common characteristic of the singing voices of teenage girls. Boys go through an obvious vocal change during puberty, but girls' voices also change, and the most obvious change is a more breathy vocal quality. This can be very annoying to a female adolescent who grew up singing. As young ladies mature, their voices will gain more tonal focus and breathiness will diminish.

An untrained singing voice can also have a breathy quality to it. Some voices require training to guide the vocal cords into complete closure. The best method to reduce breathy vocal quality, train the vocal cords to close and create more tonal focus is to sing vocal exercises on [k] and [g].

Ka ka ka ka ka on a five note descending scale (so, fa, mi, re, do).

Ga ga ga ga ga on a five note descending scale (so, fa, mi, re, do).

Tension, whether psychologically or physically induced, will affect the voice. A tense body will result in a less-than-spectacular voice and affect vocal performance.

Chapter Nine

TENSION AND THE SINGER

TENSION DIRECTLY AFFECTS THE VOICE

THEORETICALLY, ONCE A SINGER OR speaker has found his or her vocal power within the core of the body, the voice should simply release and flow freely through the vocal cords into the resonators and out of the body. In reality, anyone who has ever sung knows that this is not so easy. For most of us, the voice gets affected or altered somewhere on its journey out of the body by tensions that grip or hold the sound from freely releasing. A clear example is the shoulder girdle. Often, when new singers take a breath, they also raise the shoulders. The shoulder girdle has no need to move in breathing, but the student can unconsciously raise and tense the shoulders during inhalation. The job of the teacher is to make students aware of unnecessary muscle tension so that they can learn to breathe, activating only the muscles needed for inhalation and consciously instructing the other muscles, like the shoulder girdle, to relax.

A very important part of a voice teacher's job is to identify the parts of the body that are stopping or hindering the voice from freely releasing. The trained eyes of an experienced voice teacher can see and feel where the tensions are in the student's body. They can scan the body for tensions or blockages that are obstructing the student's voice. By eliminating tension, the student can free the voice. Sometimes, even when we consciously know that we are holding tension, we cannot release the area, because too much stress has accumulated in that part of the body.

Tension Checklist

Tension, whether psychologically or physically induced, will affect the voice. A singer or actor can greatly benefit by going through a checklist of possible places where the voice can get blocked. Starting from the top of your head, scan your body from head to toe and become aware of any parts that feel tight or tense. In master classes, students often watch a master teacher move different parts of a singer's body to miraculous results, enabling the student to sing better, instantly. A student may also learn the specific places of tension that a well-trained voice teacher will know to look for. Actors usually do body relaxation or movement exercises as a warm-up to performance; singers often do not. A tense body will result in a less-than-spectacular voice and will definitely affect vocal performance. The world of singing can benefit from the techniques available to actors today. Let's examine some of the most important places to look for tension in a performer's body.

> *The vocal cords are never to be used as a power source for the voice. They are a small vibrating part of an instrument that is much larger, similar to a reed in a clarinet.*

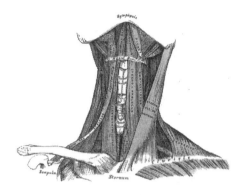

THE NECK

Look at the picture of the neck. The neck is composed of a series of strap muscles that we want to keep relaxed during phonation. Many of these muscles attach to the hyoid bone, the only free-floating bone in the body, from which the larynx hangs. The larynx is the cartilaginous structure that encases the vocal cords. Find the hyoid bone in the picture. If you put your fingers on the bottom of your chin and move backward, toward the throat, the first thing you will feel is the hyoid bone. Because the hyoid bone is free-floating, it is connected to other parts of the body, only through muscle. This makes it susceptible to any tension that creeps into the muscles of the neck. Any tension exerted on the hyoid bone can go into the larynx. Thus, neck tension can negatively influence our sound.

Let's take a look at some of the muscles attachments to the hyoid bone. Above the hyoid bone there are muscles that run from the skull, the tongue and the chin, and attach to it. These suprahyoid muscles include the digastric, stylohyoid, geniohyoid, and

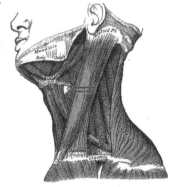

mylohyoid. One of the major muscles of the mouth, the tongue, has its bottom attachment to the hyoid bone. Voice teachers repeatedly tell singers to relax the tongue, jaw and the head because tension can travel from these muscles directly into our voice. It feels very relaxing to move the hyoid bone from side to side due to the number of muscles attached to it. Find your hyoid bone with your fingers again. Remember, it is the first thing that you will feel in the top of your neck when you move your fingers back along the base of your chin toward your throat. Put one finger on the left side of the hyoid bone and one finger on the right side and move it gently from side to side. It may make a clicking sound. Some people find moving the hyoid bone weird, but it is perfectly safe to gently move this bone. Since it is a free-floating bone, it is attached only to muscle. Moving the hyoid bone will relieve any stress that might have built up in the muscles that attach to it, and most of my students quickly get addicted to mobilizing it.

Frontal Neck Massage

After freeing up your hyoid bone, go ahead and massage the muscles on each side of the larynx and down the sides of the front of the neck. A recent doctoral study concluded that massage of the external framework of the larynx was most advantageous for voice use and vocal health.

THE RELAXED THROAT

According to Shakespeare, "The old Italian masters insisted on the throat being free and open, so that the tongue can readily and unconsciously adapt itself to the tone or pronunciation of the vowels. A remarkable agreement certainly exists between the open state of the throat and the command of the breath by the muscles inside the body; one compels the other" (1924, 18).

Many singers struggle with problems of throat constriction, especially when singing high notes. Beginning students will often engage the constrictor muscles while singing. These muscles are only to be used for swallowing, but they can engage while singing.

Right now, stop reading this book and go and get a glass of water. Take a drink of water and when you swallow, notice all the muscles that activate in your neck. We have a whole series of swallowing muscles called constrictor muscles, which squeeze the throat to guide a piece of food or liquid down the esophagus. These muscles are only to be used for swallowing, but anyone who has ever sung a high note has probably felt them engage. Many singers feel the throat close when reaching for a difficult note. To correct squeezing the throat, *open the throat* was a commonly heard statement from voice teachers of the past, but this statement can induce incorrect phonation. The yawn is often used as an example, but the yawn contains an unnecessary pharyngeal (back of throat) distention and a certain degree of tension that is unwanted in singing or speech. We can adjust the pliable walls of the pharynx as in yawning, but most voice teachers recommend not stretching the throat unnaturally open because, aside from tension, this can lead to a throaty or "woofy" sounding vocal quality. Therefore, what the voice teacher really means by an open throat is to maintain a naturally relaxed throat, without any sensation of constriction. While singing or speaking, the image of the throat widening sideways can help the student keep the throat relaxed. Shakespeare created his "whispered ahs" exercises (earlier in the book) to practice keeping the throat relaxed while singing.

Lazy Mouth Singing

I know this sounds funny, but have you ever seen people try to speak when they are drunk? Their mouth is so relaxed that they are unable to pronounce words clearly. Sing a song with lazy articulation, mimicking someone who is drunk, and see if you can feel a loose sensation all the way down into the throat. Imagine that the throat is open without stretching the circumference of the throat in any way. Play with singing different pitches this way. Notice if your sound emits more freely. Many people can reach higher pitches with lazy mouth singing.

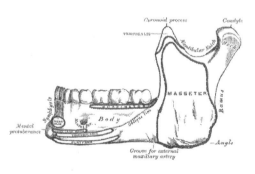

THE JAW

For voice work, it is very important to learn to relax the jaw. Many people suffer from jaw tension and any tension in the jaw can directly affect the voice. Francesco Lamperti said, "On the freedom of the jaw depends the freedom of the larynx" (Shakespeare 1924, 14). Put your fingers in front of both ears and find the temporomandibular joint, the joint between the temporal bone of the skull and the lower jaw, the mandible. Open and close your mouth. If there is some clicking, don't worry, this is normal. Chew to loosen up the jaw and massage this joint gently. Feel how the lower jaw slides forward and drops down from the groove where it is inserted.

Move your fingers on a diagonal down below your cheeks and find the masseter muscle, which closes your mouth in chewing and closing the jaw. It is the muscle that you will feel in the middle of the side of your face, between your upper and lower teeth. Beneath this muscle is a pair of deep muscles called the medial and lateral pterygoids. These muscles assist in raising and protruding the jaw and lateral movement of the jaw. These muscles are often very tight and can cause pain in the face. Massage this area with your fingertips. It may be very tender, so easy does it.

As the muscles release some of their tension, you will find it easier to keep your jaw released and relaxed for singing. Sometimes you may see a singer whose jaw shakes or jerks when he or she sings. This is an indicator of too much tension in the jaw, or too much air being pushed against the vocal cords. It is also an indicator of not enough support from the core muscles of the body. A shaking jaw is considered very bad technique and must always be avoided.

Most singers need a little more vertical space between their top and bottom teeth then is used for speaking. For singing, we want to gently increase the vertical space in our mouth, keeping some space between the back molars. Many people talk with their mouths closed and, therefore, try to sing with their mouths closed as well. Good speech often requires a larger vertical space for the mouth than we are used to, and in singing, more space is absolutely required. Since many singers and speakers hold a lot of tension in their jaw, letting the jaw remain open for a period of time can be difficult. To find this vertical space, it is best to think of adding extra space between the back molars. How wide should we keep our mouth open for singing? Some voice teachers and choral directors advocate keeping the jaw widely open or hanging it in an idiot position, the position your mouth is in when you say "duh." Some require the student to put three fingers between the top and bottom teeth and keep this vertical space while singing. Voice scientists have now discovered that requiring the jaw to stay open too widely can create excess jaw tension. Keeping the mouth too open can also remove the upper partials in a tone, which create its vocal brilliancy. So, balance is necessary. Many of the old Italian treatises required the singer to open the mouth one finger wide. Giovanni Battista Lamperti stated, "the mouth should be opened wide enough to permit the forefinger to pass between the upper and lower teeth" (1905, 6).

Pitch will affect the amount of space needed in the mouth. You will often need to increase the vertical space of your mouth as you sing higher up the scale. It can be hard to sing a very high note with a closed mouth. Also, certain pop belting styles require a wider-than-speech-sized mouth.

Molar Space Exercise

Close your mouth so that your teeth are touching. Now add a little bit of space between your back molars. Notice how your jaw has to release to create extra space between the back teeth, but your mouth is not gaping open. I have heard of teachers requiring students to put two, three and four fingers between their front teeth. Try this and see how it feels. I think three or more fingers are definitely too many; one to two fingers are more possible to sing with.

Hanging Jaw Exercise

Since many singers and speakers hold tension in their jaws, letting the jaw remain open for a period of time can be difficult. The following exercise is most helpful. Open your mouth and see if you can unhinge your jaw so that it hangs down as if you were saying "duh." Find a wine cork and put it sideways between your front and bottom teeth. Close your teeth around the cork and let the jaw stay open while checking e-mail or watching TV. (Please don't choke on the cork!)

Here is an alternative exercise you can do if you don't have a wine cork. Open your mouth widely and put your hands on each side of your face to hold your mouth open. If your jaw is tight, let the chin fall to the floor and breathe.

Jaw Singing Exercise

Put the tip of your thumb sideways between your front teeth. Say "la la la," only using the tongue to articulate the "la." Notice that the chin, jaw, face and lips do not have to move or change position as you say "la." Now, sing up the scale, higher and higher and don't let there be any movement in your chin, jaw, face or lips. Only the tongue will be moving and you will have to use your air to sing up the scale. If your thumb starts to hurt, it means that your jaw is having trouble hanging open, and I recommend doing some jaw stretching exercises. Also, this is a great exercise to do if you suffer from a shaking chin when you sing.

Humming Chewing Exercise

Chew with your mouth closed. Now hum a comfortable pitch while continuing to chew. Notice if you tighten your jaw when you add sound. If so, continue sounding and chewing, loosening your jaw. Voice scientists have actually found that the act of chewing wakes up the voice muscles. This is a terrific exercise for singers and actors (Miller, 1986, 233).

Feldenkrais Jaw Exercise

The next exercise is an exercise from Feldenkrais. Catherine Fitzmaurice taught me this exercise and it is now my favorite jaw exercise. Hold on to your chin firmly with your fingers. Without moving your arms or chin, lift your head, stretching your jaw using the top part of your head. Let the jaw stretch open. If you are seated, it is especially helpful to rest your elbows on a table or your knees so that you don't lift your arms. Remember, only use the top part of your head to open your mouth. We usually initiate movement with the chin, so stretching the jaw using the top part of the head is very relaxing.

> *Many people, especially women, hold the abdomen in all the time. If you do not release your belly, on inhalation, the diaphragm may be restricted in its movement and you may deprive yourself of a full breath.*

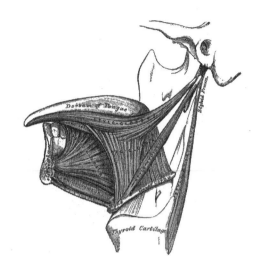

THE TONGUE

The tongue is often one of the greatest creators of tension for the singer, actor or public speaker. One of the strongest muscles in the body, the tongue can create a great deal of tension in the throat, jaw and neck areas. Shakespeare wrote, "The freedom of the tongue is indeed synonymous with the open throat; for we cannot close the throat without stiffening the tongue" (1924, 20). Many singers and speakers are completely unaware that the tongue is causing the tension they are feeling in their voice. The tongue is a much larger and more complicated organ than the part you see when you stick it out of your mouth. The only part that we can visibly see is the dorsum of the tongue. Below the top of the tongue, the anterior part of the tongue is attached to the chin bone (genioglossus). The tongue then descends into the throat, attaching on its underside to the hyoid bone (hyoglossus). The tongue also has an interesting muscle attachment to the styloid process of the temporal bone of the skull (styloglossus). So lower jaw tension and tension in the sides and base of the skull can directly affect the tongue and vice versa.

The tongue is a very flexible muscle that can change shape, depending on the sounds articulated. Many of us go to yoga and relaxation classes to stretch and relieve tension, but do we remember the tongue? We have found that when completely relaxed, the tongue will float up and rest on the roof of the mouth.

Tongue Massage

Feel the tip of your chin with your index finger. Slide your finger under your chin feeling for the bony ridge of the bottom of the chin. Keep moving your finger back, a little toward your throat and press upward. You will feel a soft area between the chin and your larynx. Stick your finger up into this soft area and massage. This is the base of your tongue. The tongue area should be soft and pliable. If the area feels taut, you probably have tongue tension, and if you massage it for a few minutes, it will become more relaxed. Singers and actors find massaging the base of the tongue under the chin pleasurable, and the result is less tongue tension.

> *The tongue is often one of the greatest creators of tension for the singer, actor or public speaker.*
> *Many singers and speakers are completely unaware that the tongue is causing the tension they are feeling in their voice.*

TONGUE EXERCISES

The Lion

Open your mouth as big as you can, stick your tongue out as far as you can and say ahhhh, like a lion roaring. Open your throat as wide as you can. This is part of a yoga posture called "The Lion."

Tongue Circles

Turn your tongue to the right. With your tongue still out of your mouth, make clockwise and counterclockwise circles. Now turn your tongue to the left and make clockwise and counterclockwise circles again. Imagine that you are licking ice cream off your lips.

Tongue Rolls

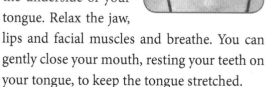

Stick your tongue out of your mouth. Roll the tip of your tongue upward against the back of your top teeth. If you look in a mirror, you will see the underside of your tongue. Relax the jaw,

lips and facial muscles and breathe. You can gently close your mouth, resting your teeth on your tongue, to keep the tongue stretched.

Roll the tip of the tongue downward against the bottom front teeth. If you look in a mirror, you will see the top of your tongue. Relax the jaw, lips and facial muscles and breathe.

The Rolled [r]

The rolled or Spanish [r] is one of the best exercises to relax both the front and very back of the tongue. In order for the flapping of the tongue to take place against the roof of the mouth, no tension can be in the muscle bundles that make up the body of the tongue. When you roll the [r], there is no tension at the top of the tongue where the tongue hits the roof of the mouth. When you roll the [r], it also creates relaxation in the base of the tongue at the attachment to the hyoid bone in your neck.

Tongue Hang

The next exercise is the most important of all. I call it, "hanging out with your tongue." Close your eyes, slightly drop your jaw and completely release the tongue muscle from its root. It may protrude out of your mouth onto your bottom front teeth. Just hang out in this position for a few minutes. You will notice that your jaw will start to release; many also notice a release in the cervical spine. This is an exercise that you can use throughout the day.

Blah Exercise

Sing a five note descending scale (so, fa, mi, re, do) on "blah." Blah, blah, blah, blah, blah.

The made-up word "blah" is fantastic to sing. It requires the jaw to hang and the tongue to release forward and downward. If you are ever having trouble singing a song, try singing it on "blah." Most people find "blah" an open, relaxing word to pronounce.

TONGUE POSITION FOR SINGING

For all vowel production the tongue should remain relaxed, touching the bottom front teeth. The tongue will change shape depending on the vowels, arching for some and flattening for others, but it should not pull away from the front teeth. Take a hand mirror or stand in front of a mirror. Relax your tongue with the tip gently resting behind your bottom teeth. Now say "ah, eh, ah, eh." Notice that the tongue slightly changes shape for each sound, but the tip of the tongue, if relaxed, stays in contact with the back of the bottom teeth. The tongue will move from this place when articulating consonants, but when singing vowels, we want it to return to the bottom of the mouth and relax. This is the goal for singing and it is also a good idea for speaking. When not relaxed, while singing, the tongue will pull back and can actually obstruct the sound of the voice as it rides outward. This can cause a throaty voice quality and alter vocal color. The tongue often tenses, thinking it can help pull the air out of the body, but it is mistaken. More often, it will obstruct airflow and cause a squeezed or blocked vocal sound. A relaxed tongue guarantees good vowel production and assists in free airflow, which leads to our goal: beautiful singing.

If your head shakes when you sing, this is a sign of poor vocal technique and is an indicator of a voice that is not core connected. Head tension will most likely accompany tension in the throat.

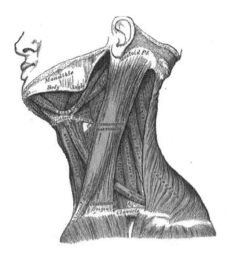

THE SKULL

The next place in our body to look for tension is the lower sides and back of the skull. Many people tense the back of the skull or lift their head when they sing. The muscles of the neck that attach to the skull can become tense and immobilize the skull during singing. There is a muscle, called the stylohyoid muscle, which travels from the styloid process of the skull, a bony process that is on each side of the head at about the level of the base of your ear, and directly attaches to the hyoid bone, from which your larynx hangs. Due to the connection of the stylohyoid muscle to the hyoid bone, tension in the sides and base of the skull can directly cause tension in the voice. This is the reason voice teachers often move the heads of singers, or tell singers to gently move their own head while they sing (in rehearsal only). For performance, we want the skull to remain floating on the top of the spine, facing forward, relaxed and unaffected by phonation. Do not lift your head when you sing. Many singers automatically lift their heads as they sing up into their higher registers. This is considered poor technique and singers need to train their heads not to move in response to pitch changes. Some people may feel that lifting the head as they sing higher helps them to reach the notes, but it actually puts the vocal tract out of good alignment for singing. Men, because they possess a larger larynx than women, will often want to lift their head to make room for the movement of the larynx. Lifting the head and any tension in the head can also be an indicator that students are not using their cores to power and support their voice.

The *eight-on-its-side* head rotation exercise in the warm-up is an excellent exercise to loosen up these muscles.

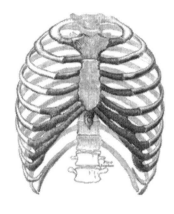

THE RIBCAGE

Inhalation is an active process. Right now, inhale through your nose. Notice that you had to initiate the inhalation and that the breath activated the diaphragm and rib muscles. Now quickly exhale. Exhalation is a passive process. The breath falls out of the body as the diaphragm and ribcage recoil to their initial positions. In singing, we want to transform the passive exhalation to an active exhalation. Singing is delaying exhalation, and to accomplish the delay, the muscles of exhalation have to become active. The major muscles that are engaged to control exhalation are the abdominal muscles and the ribcage. In times past, to strengthen the ribcage's muscles, singing teachers would have the student take a big breath and then tie a belt around the upper abdomen of the student. They would then require their students to keep the ribcage open and the upper abdomen expanded as they sang. If the student closed his ribcage during singing or final exhalation, the belt would fall down and he would be scolded. The goal of the exercise was to strengthen the costal muscles between the ribs that hold the ribcage open so that it does not torque closed, as is its habit, and to strengthen the abdominal muscles. The muscles of the chest and back that assisted the sternum in staying lifted were also strengthened, allowing the singer to be able to comfortably keep the ribcage expanded. The Italian School of Singing advocated that the singer should stay in the position of inspiration at all times, even during exhalation. This technique is still practiced today. To assist the singer in keeping the ribcage expanded, a special singer's posture, which some voice teachers call the *noble position*, is used (Miller 2004, 34). When the muscles of the student's body are strong and under his or her control, their next goal is to activate the muscles of exhalation, without any unnecessary tension. When the student has strengthened the muscles of the ribcage and can keep it comfortably open, *appoggio* can be achieved by activation of the abdominal musculature, and there will be no unnecessary tension in the ribcage. The abdominal muscles will actually help hold the ribcage open. Unnecessary tension in the ribcage can cause the singer to be unable to move freely around the stage and can also cause unnecessary tension throughout the body. Have you ever been to an opera where the singers looked stiff and static? They were probably activating too much ribcage tension.

Ribcage Exercise

Don't move your hips and try moving your ribcage left and right while singing. Now move your ribcage front and back. Move your ribcage in circles while singing. Notice if there is any change to your voice. If your voice improves, then you may have extra tension in your ribcage that you do not need.

Hang Over a Ball

A great exercise to open up the front of the body is to hang over a large exercise ball. Iyengar yoga uses large balls to stretch the ribcage and the abdominal muscles. Put the exercise ball on a yoga mat to help stabilize it. Start from a seated position at one end and slowly lean your back over the ball. When you are on the ball, see if you can stretch out your arms and legs and breathe. Try sounding in this position. Come off the ball by rolling your body down one side of the ball, returning to the beginning, seated position.

THE ABDOMEN

Remember, when the singer or actor inhales, he or she must relax the belly to allow air to drop in quickly. Many people, especially women, hold the abdomen in all the time. If you do not release your belly on inhalation, you will end up with a shallow breath. The breath will be too far away from the abdominal muscles to engage them. You will instead try to engage the throat or chest to power the voice to poor results. Our goal is to connect to the support muscles of the body without generating extra unnecessary tension in the abdomen. Once a student finds his or her abdominal support muscles, he or she may think that if some muscle engagement helps the voice, more muscle engagement will be better. This is not the case. More muscle engagement will only result in the singer working harder than is necessary to produce sound.

Yoga practitioners and athletes sometimes overdevelop their abdominal muscles to the extent that they are unable to relax their abdomens while standing. Unknowingly, their breathing has become compromised and they are unable to let go of the abdominal muscles to allow the diaphragm to lower for a deep breath. Overdeveloped abdominals may require deep massage treatments to loosen up the muscles and allow them to relax. Deep stretching of the abdominal region is also beneficial; the hanging over the ball exercise is perfect for this. Stretching of the psoas muscle is also of benefit to the singer as tightness in this muscle can affect breathing.

Try singing while lying on your back. The abdominal muscles, which are engaged to maintain an upright posture, are completely released in this position.

While doing lip buzzes or any sort of sustained singing, massage your stomach without tensing the core. Allow the voice to activate the abdominal muscles. If you are not sure how to do this, do the consonant exercises earlier in the book.

THE HIPS AND LOWER BACK

The bottom of the spine greatly affects the top of the spine. If you go to a chiropractor complaining of a neck ache, the first place he will examine is the lower spine. The spine is a support for the voice and tension in the lower spine can affect it. Some voice teachers have students clench their thighs and buttocks as a way to induce lower body support for the voice. I have heard of a teacher who uses a "thigh master" device. The idea is that if there is a lot of muscle engagement in the lower half of the torso, the abdominal musculature will be strongly engaged. This technique is now considered questionable, and although it may assist the singer in engaging support muscles, it more likely creates unnecessary tension. The result is induced muscle tension in the lower half of the body that affects breathing and can inhibit a free voice. Two of the best exercises for lower spine tension are the snake and hip circles, located in the warm-up exercises of this book.

Lower Back Exercise

Jazz dance is wonderful for flexibility of the lower back. Imagine you are a jazz dancer and rotate your pelvis from back to front, pushing your butt out and then tucking it under. After loosening up your lower back, see if you can find a place between the butt-out and pelvis-tucked-under position, where your lower half feels balanced under your top half.

THE KNEES

Pressing the knees back in what we call a locked knee position can create tension in the body and affect your breathing. Our knees are meant to be in direct alignment under our hips and above our ankle joints. If the knees are pressed backwards, they are out of alignment with the body and can cause tension problems, which restrict a free voice. There is always at least one person in a choir who gets faint from standing for a long time on risers. This is usually the person who is standing with locked knees. Locking the knees can cause tension in the throat, which can lead to breath holding.

Knee Exercise

Stand sideways next to a tall mirror. Press your knees all the way back. How does your lower back feel? How do your hips feel? Are you clenching your legs or buttocks? Does the natural curve in your back change when you lock your knees? How does your breathing feel? Now wiggle your knees while still keeping them in direct alignment under your hips. Bend the knees, noticing how this feels. Standing with a big bend in the knees could become fatiguing. Straighten your knees while looking in the mirror, but don't lock them backwards. Find the place where your knees are centered neither forward in a bend nor pressed backwards. You are now in a "soft knee" position. Check your breathing. A gentle wiggle in the knees is often enough to check to see if your knees are evenly centered over your ankle joints, yet also relaxed.

Do not squeeze the ribcage closed to try to expel extra air out of the body. Squeezing the ribcage inward will immediately create tension in the throat.

Part Three

DISCOVERING
YOUR VOCAL BEAUTY

You can increase the richness or resonance of your voice. The consonants that are most helpful in creating a resonant voice are [n], [m] and [ng].

Chapter Ten

RESONANCE

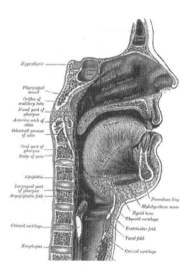

A MOUTH FULL OF SOUND

B Y ANALYZING ONE'S VOCAL SOUND, voice scientists discovered that a single sound is composed of what is called a fundamental and a series of overtones that are heard simultaneously with the fundamental. A person with a beautiful resonance or ring in his or her voice contains more overtones in the voice, and a person with a dull-sounding voice contains less overtones. By learning to use the natural resonators of the voice, we can all achieve a full vocal spectrum and use our voices to their fullest potential.

What is resonance? According to Webster's dictionary, resonance means, "the quality in a sound of being deep, full and reverberating." In voice work, we want to increase the richness or resonance in a voice. Most of us do not utilize our resonance potential. Without some sort of instruction, most people will not know how to find their full resonant voice. By adding more resonance to the voice, the voice will have more ring, richness and presence. It will also sound lower and deeper.

The resonators of the voice are the mouth cavity, the back of the throat (the pharynx), the larynx and sometimes the nose. When air hits the vocal cords, it creates a buzzing sound, which will not sound beautiful until it enters the resonators of the voice. How the voice sounds depends on where the singer allows the tone to vibrate. Have you ever looked inside your mouth? The roof of your mouth cavity arches upward like the dome of a cathedral. Everyone has a different shaped dome, and it is actually fun to look in other people's mouths to see the various shapes and sizes. Touch the roof of your mouth with your tongue. The front two-thirds of the roof of your mouth is called the hard palate and is made of bone. As you run your tongue backwards, you will come to a part of the roof of your mouth that is flexible and no longer bone. This part of your mouth is called the soft palate or velum. When you yawn, it rises. You can consciously raise your soft palate. Imagine that you are holding a beautiful rose; put this rose to your nose and smell it. Inhale through your nose and feel the soft palate arch up. If you speak without lowering the arched soft palate, you may sound British, as some British dialects use a higher soft palate for speaking than Americans.

LOWERED SOFT PALATE   **RAISED SOFT PALATE**

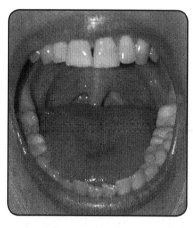 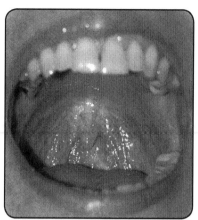

Different styles of music require different adjustments of the resonators. Opera requires a high soft palate, creating a highly arched dome in the top of the mouth, resulting in a rich, ringing resonance. Jazz does not require the soft palate to elevate and uses a mouth shape that is much more like speaking. How you choose to use your resonators will decide how much or how little resonance your voice will have. If on exhalation you let your voice go into your nose, you will create a nasal sound, which is sometimes used in country and pop music. Most voice teachers agree that nasality is to be used very sparingly, if at all. If you close off the port at the back of the soft palate by arching the soft palate (like when you smelled a rose), you will remove nasality and create more overtones in your voice, thus creating a ringing sound. Every singer or speaker needs to discover his or her resonance potential. Lack of resonance will result in a dull-sounding voice and flat tonality. If you don't like the tone of your voice, you can change it. You are not stuck with the voice you were born with.

Historically singers have used resonant voice exercises to create a beautiful sound. Many of the early treatises on the voice recommend that the singer "smell a rose" to lift the soft palate and increase resonance.

Aside from creating a more beautiful sound, using a more resonant voice is actually healthier and easier on the vocal cords. So much so that many speech pathologists use a type of speech therapy called "Resonant Voice Therapy," created by Katherine Verdolini, based on the work of Arthur Lessac. Voice scientists have found that using a resonant voice takes stress off the vocal cords and is especially useful in training speakers with voice problems.

How do we find our resonant voice? Through the use of the nasal consonants in the English language, we can improve our vocal tone. Voice trainers discovered that, by sounding on the consonants [m], [n] and [ng], singers and speakers will feel vibrations in the face. If you hum the nasal consonants, they make the voice vibrate against the hard palate of the mouth, which then radiates sympathetic vibrations into the bones of the face. Many old Italian singing treatises have called this "singing in the mask of the face," and most people feel vibration in the bones across their sinuses, the nose and the forehead, in a sort of "mask" area.

Why do we feel the bones in our face vibrate? Stick your thumb in your mouth and rest it on the roof of your mouth. Now hum a tone close to the pitch you normally speak on and feel with your thumb the vibrations on the roof of your mouth. Try a lower tone. You should feel the whole roof of your mouth vibrating. These vibrations of sound hitting your hard palate will continue outwards, into the bones of your face. Now hum a low tone that vibrates your whole hard palate and hum up the scale. You will notice that only part of the hard palate vibrates as you get higher and, as you go up the scale, vibration on the hard palate moves gradually backwards. Different pitches will radiate out into different parts of the face and head, depending on where the air hits the hard and soft palate. The low- and mid-range notes tend to vibrate the singer's whole mask area. For the higher notes up the scale, most singers feel vibration in the forehead, and for the very highest notes, singers, especially sopranos, often feel the vibration of sound going out the top or back of the head. These sensations are subtle and it takes time for some people to experience them. So, do not be alarmed if you do not have any sensation in your face or head at first, and the idea of vibrations of sound radiating through your face sounds like a fantasy. As you become more aware of the nuances surrounding your newfound voice, these vibrations will become more defined. One of the easiest ways to start feeling these new vibrations is to hum different pitches and put your fingers on the bridge of the nose, the bones of your cheeks, in your eye sockets and on the back of your neck. Explore where your body vibrates when you make sounds.

Singing often produces the sensation of having a mouth full of sound. If you do not feel any parts of your face vibrate when you sing, notice the sensation of air against the roof of your mouth. Where do you feel the air in your mouth when you create a beautiful sound? Often a student will not know when he is producing a beautiful sound. That is why a voice teacher is necessary. A voice teacher acts as an external ear to let you know when  you are producing an aesthetically pleasant sound and instructs you on how to consistently replicate these sounds.

What type of tone you make depends on how you couple your resonators. Coupling means how you combine the percentage of mouth to nasal to throat resonance that you use. You can modify how your voice sounds depending on how you modify your resonators. Each speaker, actor or singer must find his or her resonance, and it is actually fun. Very few people truly have ugly voices. You are not stuck with the voice you were born with and can add as little or as much resonance to your voice as you desire. Resonance work is equally important for actors as well as singers. An actor has to be able to embody different characters, each of which will possess a different voice. So, the actor needs to be aware of all the resonant possibilities for the voice, from very nasal and ugly, to very beautiful.

DOWNWARD DOG SOUNDING

Get into the yoga position, downward dog. Make some easy sighing sounds and let gravity assist your voice in moving through your body. You will notice that the voice will fall into the head. Do not try to get the sound to emit from the mouth or throat. In downward dog, the voice will fall into the head cavity, which is where the resonators of the voice are located. Try gliding up and down the scale and pick a pitch that feels effortless to sing. High pitches are the easiest in this posture. Try humming on that pitch and notice the vibration of sound in the head. Now sing a woooo, sliding up the scale to the highest note you can hit. It is normal to feel a lot of pressure in your head when you sing a high note in this posture. After experimenting with singing high notes in downward dog, come to a standing posture and see if you can sing the same high notes, allowing the voice to fly up into the head. There should still be a sensation of pressure in the head. When the sound reaches the hard palate in the mouth, the bones of the skull vibrate, turning you literally into a bell-head.

THE SOUND COLUMN

While singing, many perform-ers experience the sensation of having a channel or column of air to sing on. This is not a scientific fact, there is no actual column of air in the body; it is only a sensation. Directing the air to the hard and soft palate at the roof of the mouth balances the air pressure coming from below. Without a clear idea of what sort of sound you want and where you want to send it, the result will probably be what feels like an unstable sound column. Singers and speakers experience a sensation of sound originating in their abdominal region, or all the way down in the base of their pelvis. They then experience sound ending inside their head. Having the sensation of a beginning and ending place of sound helps the singer or speaker have a steady, even voice. An unstable sound column can result in flat singing and lack of tonal focus. Many American singers struggle with this. The American dialect uses a relaxed soft palate and the language tends to roll off the top of the tongue, never coming in contact with the hard palate at the roof of the mouth. There can also be a tendency to try to push the voice out of the throat if the singer or speaker does not feel the air ending or vibrating in their head. Obviously, the voice cannot exit the body from the throat, but without a top surface (the hard palate) for the voice to bounce off of, a singer or speaker will often try to push the voice out of the throat.

ANOTHER WAY FOR VOCAL ONSETS

The onset of a tone can be approached in two ways. We can start a tone with the sensation of the voice in the abdominal musculature, or we can start a tone with a hum on [m], feeling the vibration of the voice in the resonators. Some classical singers will start a high note with a soft hum and gradually add more voice until they create a full tone. The best onset of tone uses a balance of both. I like vocal onset exercises that start with [me] better, instead of the more common [he]. There is less of a chance of hitting the vocal cords together on the production of vowels when the resonators are engaged.

STRAW EXERCISE

The straw is terrific to sound in if you are having trouble feeling any vibrations of resonance in your face. I make all my students practice with straws to find their resonance potential. Take your plastic drinking straw and put it in your mouth. Hum a low or speaking level pitch into the straw and notice all the buzzing vibrations you feel in your lips and face. Take the straw out and hum the same note. See if you can still feel the vibrations in your face. Put the straw back in your mouth and hum a [mm] to [uh]. See if you can keep the richness of the tone in the vowel sound. Now take the straw out and still hum a [mm] to a [uh], still producing a rich resonant tone. The sensations of vibration may be subtler without the straw.

EXERCISES FOR RESONANCE

The consonants that are most helpful in creating a resonant voice are [n], [m] and [ng]. Imagine that you are smelling a beautiful rose and inhale, letting the soft palate rise. Now say an [m], [n], [ng]. Speak the following sentences, paying attention to the vibrations in the front of your face. Your lips may also tickle with vibration. Do not allow the sound to go nasal. If you are singing with nasality, the nose will feel stuffed up, as if you have a cold, and the sound will not be beautiful. If you are using your resonant voice, your nose will vibrate with air and the sound will ring. The sensation is almost like you are singing up your nose, and before body imaging, some voice teachers thought that this was the case. E.G. White wrote a book in 1909 called *Science and Singing*, stating that sound was completely made in the sinuses and not by the vocal cords. His theory was based on the sensations experienced in singing. His theory was disproved by the advent of x-ray technology. There is one person advertising on the Internet who still mistakenly teaches his technique.

In singing, it is best to use the Italian method of saying an [n], [m] and [ng]. In English, we use our lips to say an [m], but in Italian, an [m] is a hum. In English, we touch the tip of our tongue to the roof of the mouth to say an [n], but in Italian, an [n] is also a hum. In singing, whenever you have an [n], [m] or an [ng], always hum on them. Also, try humming the nasal consonants when you speak and your speaking voice will instantly be richer.

Speak or sing the following sentences while humming on the nasal consonants and notice the rich resonance that this produces. Try to maintain the same degree of resonance on both nasal and non-nasal consonants and the vowels.

Many monkeys
Money money money
Mime mime mime
Many minions mingle
Nime nime nime
Gnomes live in Nome
Mary mooches Mona's money
Mom made marmalade
My oh my, Minnie's moody
Merry monkeys march madly

Marshmallows mostly melt
Nona needs Nancy's needles
Mimes make Nanna nervous
Sing, sing, a ling, a ling
Gnome, gnome, gnome
Knock, knock

Italian Words

Mamma

Luna

Mio

L'anello

Montalcino

Mangiare

Andiamo

Paragraph for Practice

Mary made a marmalade jam sandwich for her cousin Nancy, and they marched in the moonlight of the full moon on the moor to the home of their ancestor's bones. The mature elm tree leaned lightly over the majestic monoliths in the cemetery. A nervous mockingbird sang a nighttime song, singing so sensitively that Mary and Nancy kneeled at the foot of the elm. While kneeling on their knees in the moss, they suddenly heard the strangest sounds coming from behind the largest tombstone. The sound of a moaning man, clanging metal and military marching men rang in the night. Mary nervously nudged Nancy toward the largest monolith from which the sound was emanating. Their knees nervously knocked and suddenly the mockingbird flew from the elm toward them, nearly knocking them down. "Who comes in the night?" a male baritone voice asked.

Resonant Voice into Regular Speech

Once you can make a rich sound using the resonant consonants [m], [n] and [ng], try to keep the same sensation of resonance that you have on a resonant sentence and say a regular sentence. Eventually, you will be able to train your voice to keep a rich tone on all vowel and consonant combinations.

Gnomes live in Nome. Where are you going?

Zing Singing Exercise

On any pitch, sing "zing," letting the sound ring and then carry that ringing resonance into the following vowel. You may feel the velopharyngeal port (opening into the sinuses) flip closed as you go from the [ng] to the vowel.

Zing ee

Zing eh

Zing ah

Zing oh

Zing oo

Resonant Chant

A favorite resonant exercise of famous voice teacher Richard Miller was the use of two Italian words (1986, 87):

"Ogni uomo." Phonetically, "awn-ye womo."

Sing these two words over and over on one pitch, like a chant, and see how much resonance you can create in your voice.

TO REMOVE NASALITY

Sometimes a person has a soft palate that does not close completely, resulting in a voice with a nasal quality. The student will need to practice exercises to strengthen the closing of the velopharyngeal port. The velopharyngeal port is the entrance into the sinus cavities. This opening is closed when the velum (soft palate) lifts upward and backward, like a flap, touching the back wall of the throat. The best word to use is *hunga*. Say *hunga* and notice how the *"hung"* makes a nasal sound, but when you say the *"ga,"* there is movement in the back of your mouth. The movement that you feel is the velum lifting, thus closing off the soft palate.

Nasal singing is often confused for the forward, ringing vocal sound that is popular in pop music today. Most singers are trying to get the voice to vibrate forward in the mouth, with the velum port entrance to the sinuses closed. I often see young students sing in their sinuses, thinking that sinus singing is beautiful singing. They try to mimic pop singers without any real understanding of voice training. Alicia Keys and other pop singers sometimes wiggle their noses when they sing to get the air up to the roof of the mouth and vibrating into the bones of their face. An untrained singer might interpret nose wiggles as sinus singing. People who sing nasally are, also, often not connected to the core support of their body. Good singing is always core-connected; otherwise, the voice will have no depth or power to it. Some singers, especially country singers, use some nasality to get a "twang" in the voice. The use of too much nasality will reduce the singer's vocal power, as the voice can get stuck in the nose. If you want a country western sound, use as little nasality as possible. If you use too much nasality, you will decrease your vocal power. A little bit of nasality goes a long way.

BHRAMARI PRANAYAMA

One of my favorite pranayama exercises to help students become aware of head resonance is *bhramari* pranayama. *Bhramara* means a black bumblebee. Lie down or sit in a chair and close your eyes. *Bhramari* pranayama is practiced by raising the elbows to shoulder level and putting the hands on the face in a position called *sanmukhi mudra*. Put your forefinger on your eyelids to block out light and the middle finger on the bridge of your nose, touching the finger above, to assist in blocking out light and to help you feel vibration on the bridge of the nose when you begin chanting. Place the ring finger on the side of your nostrils, and lightly press to slightly close the nasal passages. Let the pinky rest on the skin above your mouth and press your thumbs against the flesh at the front of the ears to close out external sound. Slowly inhale through the nose, filling the lungs from the bottom up. Instead of exhaling breath, hum a comfortable tone with the mouth closed, keeping space between your back teeth, until your lungs are empty. Repeat. Feel the vibration of sound on your face and inside your mouth. Listen to the sound within your head and enjoy.

Bhakti yoga is the yoga of devotion. Singing the Hindu names of God is the form of meditation praticed by Bhakti yoga devotees called japa.

Chapter Eleven

YOGA TONING

OM SHANTI

YOGA TONING IS GREAT FOR the voice and calming for the mind. Since the beginning of time, sound has played an important part in all world religions. John 1:1 in the Bible states, "In the beginning was the Word and the Word was with God and the Word was God." The Egyptians supposedly were able to levitate objects with sound. Pythagoras and the early Greek mathematicians felt that sound was extremely important to health and harmony.

In Hinduism and Yoga traditions, *Om*, or *Aum*, is the sound of the universe and all that is. It is the cosmic sound that all sound comes from and returns to. Toning is sustaining a sound on one pitch. It is similar to singing on one note and anyone can do it. If you tone *Om*, you merge your physical body with your spiritual body. Yogis even believe that you can reach enlightenment through chanting.

CHANTING OM, AUM

Sit cross-legged on the floor or in a comfortable chair and keep your spine straight. The word *Om*, when broken down, divides into three main sounds: A, U and M. Inhale from your core and start the Ah sound in the back of the mouth, bring the sound forward into the mouth for UU and close the lips for the MM, feeling the sound vibrate the bones along your cheeks, nose and forehead. See if you can wake up the third eye, also known as the sixth chakra (the area between and just above the eyebrows). When a singer is able to feel the vibration of sound in the third eye, the result is a beautiful tone with a complete spectrum of overtones. In addition to being great for your soul, chanting also has the benefit of increasing one's awareness of subtle sensations that, when felt, contribute to beautiful tone.

CHAKRA CHANTING AND MEDITATION

In yoga, there is an energy channel that runs from the base of our body all the way up the spine and out the head. At certain strategic points in the body, we have energy centers called chakras. Chakra means wheel, and at each energy center, a chakra is represented as a lotus blossom with a variety of petals. The chakras can open like a flower and spin when sound is directed into them. Singers often discover that by moving tones from the base of the pelvis up and out the body, they feel the sensation of the sound column that stretches from the base of their body upward and out through the top of their head. Certain pitches, when sung, naturally vibrate in certain parts of the body. Low pitches and open vowels naturally gravitate to the bottom of the torso, and as the pitches get higher up the scale and vowels become more closed, the focal point of sound vibration rises in the body. Singers and chanters often have the experience of having sound massage the inside of their body, a delicious experience. Singing, when unblocked, will naturally open up all the chakras, and a singer can experience energy flowing freely from the root chakra all the way out the crown chakra. Singers, even without an understanding of the chakras, can have the experience of sound coming from their pelvic floor, vibrating up their spine, resonating in their head and flowing out the top of their head.

MEDITATION

The following is a chanting and chakra visualization meditation. Each chakra has a one-word chant in Sanskrit, called a *bija*, with a specific pitch that you will tone on. A *bija* means seed. A *bija* mantra is the seed sound of each chakra, that when chanted, will activate the energy of the chakra.

Below the *bija* chant, I have put the actual musical note that you can chant on if you have access to an instrument. If you don't have access to an instrument, pick a mid-range, speech level tone to sound on. Use a note that is comfortable and used in your everyday speaking pattern.

Visualize a golden light coming up from the center of the earth entering into your feet, radiating up your legs and entering into the base of your pelvis.

1st *Muladhara* (base)
At the very base of the pelvis, the space between the genitals and

the anus (the perineum) lies the first chakra, the *Muladhara.* The *Muladhara* is a red lotus with four petals. Visualize the color red and open up the lotus while chanting.

Chant: Lam

Musical Note: Deep C

2nd *Svadhisthana* (sacral)

Bring the light up to just above the pubic bone and below the navel. Visualize an orange six-petal lotus. As the lotus opens, see the crescent moon in the white center of the lotus.

Chant: Vam

Musical Note: D

3rd *Manipura* (solar plexus)

Move the light up to the solar plexus, the area above the navel and below the breastbone. See the ten-petal lotus in yellow.

Chant: Ram

Musical Note: E

4th *Anahata* (heart)

Move the light up to the heart region. See the green twelve-petal lotus in the center of your heart.

Chant: Yam

Musical Note: F

5th *Vishuddha* (throat)

Vishuddha means purification. Bring the light up to the throat. See the turquoise blue, sixteen-petal lotus flower. The throat chakra is a bridge. It takes us from one side of the river of life to the other side, into the spiritual realms. It is a passageway from earth to spirit, from the energy centers of the body to the higher energy centers of spirit.

HAPTER ELEVEN · YOGA TONING

Energy is never to sit or stop in the throat chakra. Energy rising from the breath is to keep moving through the fifth chakra, up into the sixth chakra and out the top of the head, the crown chakra.

Chant: Ham

Musical Note: G

6th *Ajna* (third eye)

Bring the light to the space between your eyebrows. Visualize two deep blue lotus petals. Let the lotus begin to spin clockwise and turn into a silver disc.

Chant: Om

Note: Musical A

7th *Sahasrara* (crown)

Bring the light from the forehead to the crown of the head. Visualize, seated on the top of your head, a glowing white thousand-petal lotus bathed in a field of violet light.

Chant: Om

Musical Note: B

Feel the violet light expand out and around your whole body, healing and cleansing. Bring the violet light back to the top of your head. Transform the violet light to white light and send it upward as far as you can, into the universe and out to all that is.

BHAKTI YOGA: MANTRAS AND KIRTAN

Bhakti Yoga is the yoga of devotion. Chanting the Hindu names of God is used as a form of meditation practiced by Bhakti yoga devotees and is called *japa*. Mantras are Indian prayers in Sanskrit that, when chanted repeatedly, still the mind, open the heart and allow one to enter into a deep state of calm and oneness with God.

In the Hindu religion, there is only one God. However, many different aspects of this one God are worshipped in song. Each aspect is called a deity. Each mantra has a presiding deity and possesses a *bija*, or sound seed, which fills the mantra with divine energy. The Bhakti Yoga devotee believes that by constant prolonged repetition of the mantra, the essence of the divine deity is revealed, thus allowing pure consciousness to be attained. Some mantras are practiced as many as 125,000 times. A devotee may have a special mantra that was originally passed down by a guru or sage, or one may also use more commonly known mantras as daily prayers. Early Christian music was based on the use of chants as well. Chants exalting the glory of God were used in the first Christian churches as part of daily worship, lifted from the practice of chanting in the Jewish synagogues before the time of Christ. Many of the early chants, such as the Kyrie, Gloria and Sanctus, are still used as part of the Christian mass today.

Sing within the temple that is your body.
By letting your voice resonate within, you will
increase the richness and power of your voice and
draw the audience toward you.

Kirtan is a form of group Bhakti devotional chanting that uses mantras. This is a fabulous vehicle for discovering your resonance while singing in community with others. The chants are usually very simple and easy for the beginning singer to follow. Kirtan is practiced in a "call and response" style. A leader will first sing the chant and then the group will answer back, repeating the chant. The leader usually plays a small portable piano called a harmonium. Sometimes other musicians accompany the kirtan leader. Many yoga studios offer kirtan, and this is a great way to practice your singing.

Although many mantras have melodies, you can chant any of the following mantras on one note of your choosing, or you may find yourself creating a melody as you chant. If a melody pops into your mind, go with it and explore it. You may be creating your own heart's song. If you would like to learn more kirtan chants, there are many authentic Indian versions available on YouTube. The authentic Indian melodies and rhythms of these chants have been passed down for centuries and are believed to hold transcendental cosmic energy.

Some chants to explore are:

Om Shanti Shanti

(*Om* Peace, Peace of God.) This mantra is chanted to feel the peace of God.

Om Namah Shivaya

(*Om* and salutations to *Shiva* and all that I am capable of becoming.) This chant is a very popular mantra and has a strong transformative effect on the mind of the individual reciting it. It is chanted to lead us to the highest state of peace and meditation. *Shiva* is responsible for change and rebirth and the shedding of old habits. *Shiva* is often pictured sitting on a tiger skin meditating in the mountains, with serpents, representing kundalini energy, wrapped around his neck.

Om Sri Rama Jaya Rama, Jaya, Jaya Rama

(*Om* and victory to *Rama,* victory, victory to *Rama.*) *Rama* is an incarnation of *Vishnu,* the supreme creator of all. He incarnated on Earth and married *Sita,* and was the perfect embodiment of a responsible and righteous husband, the perfect man. Mahatma Gandhi chanted this mantra for sixty years. This mantra is chanted to cleanse karma and transform our human nature from animal to divine.

Om Gum Ganapatayei Namaha

(*Om* and salutations to the remover of obstacles, *Ganesha,* for which *Gum* is the seed.) *Ganesha* is a deity represented as an elephant. He is the Lord of knowledge and wisdom. His name is chanted to remove difficulties.

Om Shrim Mahalakshmiyei Swaha

(*Om* and salutations to the embodiment of feminine energy, the deity *Lakshmi,* who bestows all manner of wealth, and for which *Shrim* is the seed.) *Lakshmi* is the goddess of wealth and beauty, pictured as a beautiful woman standing in a lotus blossom with her arms open and giving. This mantra is practiced to attract prosperity and wealth of all kinds, including friends and family as well as material abundance.

Om Dum Durgayei Namaha

(*Om* and salutations to the deity *Durga,* full of feminine energy, who protects us from all manner of negative influences, and for which *Dum* is the seed.) *Durga* represents the motherhood aspect of God. She has great power and is the protector of all. She is usually pictured riding a tiger. Her eight arms carry flowers and weapons of protection, while giving gestures of blessings. This mantra can be used to call upon *Durga* for protection.

Om Aim Saraswatyai Namah

(Prostrations to Mother *Saraswati* of which *Aim* is the seed.) *Saraswati* is the goddess of education, arts and music. People in the arts often worship *Saraswati* to bestow creative knowledge and talent.

Om Sri Hanumate Namah

(*Om* and prostrations to Blessed *Hanuman*.)

Hanuman is the deity represented as a monkey and is considered to be the perfection of devotion. He possesses great strength and courage and is the greatest and humblest devotee of *Lord Rama*. The *Hanuman* mantra is chanted to help one overcome fear and gain courage.

The Gayatri Mantra

Aum bhur bhuwah svah, tat savitur varenyam bhargo devasaya dhimahi dhiyo yo nah pracodayat.

A literal translation of the *Gayatri* is: "May we attain that excellent glory of *Savitar* the god, so may he stimulate our prayers."

Another less literal translation of the mantra is: "Oh God! Thou art the giver of life, remover of pain and sorrow and the bestower of happiness. Oh! Creator of the universe, may we receive thy supreme sin-destroying light. May thou guide our intellect in the right direction."

The *Gayatri Mantra* is the foremost mantra and prayer in Hinduism. It is chanted for protection, to increase wisdom and to inspire spiritual growth. The oldest known mantra, it is considered to be the most powerful of all. It is based on a *Sanskrit* verse from a hymn in the sacred book the *Rigveda*. *Krishna* said to *Arjuna* in the sacred Hindu text, *The Bhagavad-Gita*, "Among all the mantras, I am the *Gayatri*." The complete chant is to be done on one breath and the ideal times for chanting the mantra are three times a day, at dawn, midday and at dusk. The maximum benefit of chanting this mantra is achieved by chanting it 108 times. However, one may chant it for 3, 9 or 18 times when pressed for time. The syllables of the mantra are said to positively affect all the chakras in the human body.

There are numerous mentions of the *Gayatri Mantra* in the *Upanishads*, the sacred texts of Hinduism. My favorite reference to the mantra is in the *Brahadaranyaka Upanishad* 5.14.4. The *Gayatri Mantra* is called the protector of breath in this text. Maybe that is why the mantra is to be chanted on one breath.

"The *Gayatri Mantra* is based on truth. For truth is based on strength. Strength is breath, and is based on breath. So, *Gayatri* protects (*tra*) the wealth (*gaya*), which is the breath of those who speak it with earnestness and devotion. When one recites *Gayatri* on behalf of someone, it protects that person's breath as well!"

SING IN YOUR TEMPLE

There is something very Zen about singing. This is one of the reasons voice work is so fascinating. If you change your voice, you can truly change your life. The more you connect with your voice and become one with it, the more your confidence, peace and sense of personal power increases. There is a fine line between "doing" and "not doing" in singing. We want to engage certain muscles, but at the same time, let the voice release. If the singer tries too hard to get the voice out of the body, the singer will push the voice and the voice will sound small and compressed. Instead, the more you just let go and allow your voice to release from the center of your body, the freer, fuller and louder it will be. Let yourself be a sound fountain! Let the voice leave your body with the feeling of a release. Do not try to push the voice out of your body. Your voice that is vibrating within you is big enough. Let it be the size that it is right now. The voice will get bigger and stronger as you develop its muscles. Opera singers never think of throwing their voices out toward the audience. The air pressure involved in opera singing is so intense that, if this was done, the singer's throat could contract and this contraction might induce a cough. Instead, opera singers think of drawing their audience toward them, so they never think of projecting the voice outward. They let their voices resonate in their body, becoming a sound temple and, thereby, drawing the audience toward them.

Speaking and singing require more energy than most people expect. They both require an active state of readiness in the body.

Part Four

INCORPORATING
LANGUAGE

The combination of two vowels in a word is called a diphthong. When singing a diphthong, we always want to prolong the pronunciation of the first vowel, minimize the length of the second vowel and voice it quickly at the end of the word as if it were an ending consonant.

Chapter Twelve

VOWELS

SINGERS ARE VOWEL HUGGERS

MOST VOICE TEACHERS REFER TO good singing as good vowel production. The vowels carry the air and sound without interruption. The integrity of vowel production is of paramount importance in good singing. In speaking, the consonants need to be clearly articulated for good diction. In singing, we also want clear consonant articulation, but we are especially concerned with vowel production, so much so that singers could be called vowel huggers. Each vowel adjusts the vocal organs and mouth cavity into a distinctive shape, which produces a specific tone. Some vowels create a closed space in the mouth cavity and some create an open space. The goal of the singer is to produce a consistent vocal sound, from the most closed vowel to the most open vowel, regardless of the variance in mouth cavity shape. When a singer is able to sing, maintaining tonal unity from vowel to vowel, the listener hears a polished voice. If each vowel has a different vocal quality, then the listener will interpret the voice as being inconsistent and untrained.

THE VOWELS

In elementary school, we were told that the vowels of English are A, E, I, O, U and sometimes Y. However, when we closely investigate the English language, we discover that there is actually a wider variety of vowels that fall in between A, E, I, O, U.

Tongue Vowels

There are five vowels that we call the tongue vowels in singing, because the only organ that is used to articulate each of these vowels is the tongue. To make these vowels, the tongue remains sitting in the bottom of the mouth, touching the back of the bottom teeth. The lips remain relaxed and the jaw relaxes to allow an adequate mouth opening. Keeping the mouth open, sound each of the tongue vowels below. Notice that they are made by the tongue slightly changing shape in its resting position in the bottom of the mouth, without any need for movement of the lips or jaw.

A (AH)   as in FATHER
A   as in RAT
E   as in MET
I   as KIT
EE   as in SEE

The EE Vowel

The biggest adjustment, from speaking to singing, required is the pronunciation of the EE [i] vowel, as in the word need or we. In singing, we want a more vertically open mouth to produce what we call the singer's EE, as opposed to the narrow, horizontal mouth shape that we use to say EE while speaking. Speak the EE vowel. Notice that the shape of the mouth is narrow and horizontal, with very little space between the back molars. Now sing an EE vowel, maintaining that shape. What you will hear is an unattractive, possibly nasal vowel. Because of the vocal quality that the EE vowel possesses, we often modify it to make it more beautiful and to make it sound more like the other more vertical vowels of English. So, say an AH vowel and, without changing the shape of the mouth, say an EE. Notice that the EE sounds darker and rounder. This is the EE we prefer for singing. It will blend better with the rest of the vowels the singer uses.

Lip Vowels

In the production of lip vowels, the tongue hardly moves. It remains in the lower half of the mouth, touching the back of the bottom teeth. The lips also barely move but are allowed to relax and slightly protrude. The jaw moves gently from a more open to a closed position to create the lip vowels.

A (AW) as in FALL
UR as in BURN
U as in COULD
OO as in GOOSE

Neutral Vowels

These are the most relaxed vowels. They require little use of the tongue or lips. They are similar to the sound that happens if you open your mouth and say duh.

UH as in APPLY
UH as in CUP

VOWEL COMBINATIONS

Many vowels that we hear in Standard English are actually a blending of two or more vowels. However, when singing a word that contains a combination of vowels, each vowel does not receive equal time or emphasis. A combination of two vowels in a word is called a diphthong. When singing diphthongs, we always want to enunciate the first vowel in the combination, sing on it and minimize the second vowel, voicing it at the end of the word as if it were an ending consonant.

A singer may not notice that a word contains two vowels until he or she has to sing it. However, when a singer has to sing a word like I, it will be clear that this very short word actually contains two vowels, "AH" and "EE." Does the singer hold the "AH" vowel or the "EE" vowel in the word? Many singers for whom English is not their first language will try to give equal time to each vowel or hold the second vowel longer than the first. Try doing this both ways. You will notice how funny it sounds to not lengthen the first vowel. If you hold the second vowel the longest, you will produce a word that sounds like "ah-eeeeeeeeeeeeeeeeee." This sounds very funny and not like the word I at all.

Diphthongs

Diphthongs are combinations of two vowels.

AH + EE	as in I
AH + EE	as in LIGHT
AY + EE	as in SAY
AW + I	as in FOIL
AH + OO	as in FOUND
AW + O	as in MOW
A + UR	as in PEAR
EE + UR	as in REAR

Triphthongs

Triphthongs are words with a combination of three vowels. When singing triphthongs, we always want to enunciate the first vowel in the word, sing on it and minimize the second and third vowel, quickly voicing them at the end of the word as if they were an ending consonant, like the "T" on cat. For example: the word "our" would be sung "ahhhhhhhhhh-ur."

AH + OO + UR   as in FLOUR
AH + OO + UR   as in OUR
AH + EE + UR   as in FIRE

The articulators of the mouth are the lips, the teeth and the tongue. Ineffective articulation will compromise clear communication.

Chapter Thirteen

CONSONANTS

THE LIPS, THE TEETH, THE TIP OF THE TONGUE

AN ACTOR, PUBLIC SPEAKER OR singer must learn to articulate consonants by means of clear agile approaches to, and departures from, the articulatory positions. Without clear consonant articulation, the speaker or singer will not be understood. Most of us who speak English as our first language take the articulation of consonants for granted. In order to speak with good diction, it is advantageous for the individual to review the actual method in which each consonant is produced.

The articulators of the mouth are the lips, the teeth and the tongue. They work in a variety of ways to pronounce consonants. Consonants are divided into groups denoting the method in which the articulators are used to pronounce them.

Labials (lips alone)

The labial consonants require the lips to round or come together to make sound.

m   mother
p   pie
b   bee

Labial Velar (lips and soft palate)

A labial velar consonant is articulated with both the lips and the velum (soft palate).

w   win
wh which

Labiodental (lips and teeth)

The labiodental consonants require the top teeth to touch the bottom lip in order to articulate them.

f   father
v   very

Dental (tongue and teeth)

These consonant sounds are the most difficult for non-English speakers to pronounce. To make the [th] sound the speaker or singer must slide the tip of the tongue along the bottom surface of the top teeth.

th thick
th that

Alveolar (tip of tongue and alveolar ridge)

Alveolar consonants require the tip or the blade of the tongue to touch the bony ridge, called the alveolar ridge, just above the top teeth.

t   tack
d   down
n   no
l   light
s   sell
z   zoo
r   rescue

Postalveolar (tip of tongue and hard palate)

These consonants require the tip or the blade of the tongue to connect with the back of the alveolar ridge.

sh   ship
zh   fuzion

Palatal (body of tongue and hard palate)

To make a palatal consonant the the body of the tongue needs to raise and touch the hard palate.

y   yellow

Velar (Body of tongue and soft palate)

The following consonants require the back of the tongue to articulate with the soft palate at the back of the roof of the mouth.

c   cat
k   kook
g   go
ng   sing

Glottal

The consonant h is a special consonant; it is made by air passing through the vocal cords and has no voiced sound.

    h   hat

Voiced and Unvoiced Consonants

Consonants are further divided into categories depending on whether they are voiced or unvoiced. Voiced consonants are consonants that are made with the vocal cords engaged, thus creating sound. Unvoiced consonants are consonants that are clearly articulated but do not engage the vocal cords to make sound; therefore, these consonants only make a breathy sound.

    Voiced Consonants (with vibration of vocal cords creating sound)
    b, d, g, v, th, z, w, m, n, l, r, y, ng, j, zh

    Unvoiced Consonants (no vocal cord vibration)
    c, k, p, t, ch, f, th, s, sh, wh, h

Nasal Consonants

The consonants m, n and ng are also called nasal consonants. They are called nasal consonants because the nasal passages are activated during their pronunciation.

Both Voiced and Unvoiced Pronunciation

There are a few consonants that have both voiced and unvoiced pronunciations.

    w   willow and who
    th those and theatre

CONSONANT EXERCISES

Consonant articulation exercises are fun and effective to exercise the articulators, the lips, the teeth and the tongue. Most speakers and singers will benefit by doing the following exercises to perfect their diction.

Labial Exercises (lips)

Voiced

m   My mother may swim in the Mississippi mud.
b   Betty Babcock bit the big baboon's big brown bony behind.

Unvoiced

p   The pelican's pouch is practical primarily for putting supper.

Labial Velar Exercises (lips and soft palate)

Voiced

w   The willow wilted and the weather whipped the wind wet and wild.

Unvoiced (sounds like h)

wh Who read the whole who-dun-nit?

Labiodental Exercises (top teeth to bottom lip)

Voiced

v   Vivacious vagabonds strove to give more value to the various verbs.

Unvoiced

f   Five elephants huffed and puffed as they flat-footed through the Friday fish fry.

Dental (tongue and teeth)

Voiced

th   They know that the weather withers the wooden paths.

Unvoiced

th   He thought that thin Theodore's theatrics were ruthless and unhealthy.

Alveolar (tip or blade of tongue to ridge above top teeth)

Voiced

d   Day after day the daffodils dance dreamily.

n   Nancy needs no notice when Nona, the night nurse, needs help.

l   Lulu and Larry played lovely lutes while lying in lounge chairs.

r   Rigorous rowing creates ripples in the Russian River.

z   The zebras at the Zanzibar zoo were zealous.

Unvoiced

t   It is time to try to take Terry traveling, even though Terry is two.

s   Sally Smith sits and sings songs sweetly on the swing-set in Savannah.

Postalveolar (tip of tongue and back of alveolar ridge)

Voiced

zh   A lack of supervision, confusion and delusion caused Zsa Zsa to fail.

Unvoiced

sh   Sheffield shepherds shear their shaggy sheep in the shade.

Palatal (body of tongue and hard palate)

Voiced

y Yes, yesterday I used the yellow yardstick to measure the yellow yarn.

Velar (Body of tongue and soft palate)

The following consonants require the top of the middle of the tongue to articulate with the soft palate at the back of the roof of the mouth.

Voiced

g "Go get green Gatorade for the gym," said the gorgeous girl.
ng Swimming, surfing, sunbathing and dreaming and are my favorite things to do.

Unvoiced

k The kooky cat cared for the cranky kittens.

SCAT SINGING FOR CONSONANT ARTICULATION

Jazz singers like to improvise while singing songs. They use syllables called scat syllables instead of words. Scat syllables are sounds that the vocalist uses to mimic other instruments, especially horns. Singing on scat syllables can be very freeing and can also stimulate creativity. Scatting is also an excellent and fun way to improve diction, and my favorite way to teach consonant articulation.

Below are some scat phrases to play with.

Speak the phrase and see how you need to shape your mouth for each phrase. See if there is a certain rhythm that the phrase wants to fall into. Do you naturally want to hold one syllable longer than another? Do some of the syllables want to roll quickly off your tongue or be held out? Try chanting the phrase. Do certain syllables want to go up or down in pitch? Do you want to repeat any part of the phrase? Try putting some of the phrases together. Pick an easy song and instead of singing the words, sing scat phrases. See if any of the phrases spark your creativity and assist you in creating your own syllables or melodies. There is no wrong or right in scat singing. Listen to a jazz record with a horn instrumentalist. See if any of the sounds the horn makes sound like scat syllables. Notice how the horn player alters the melody creating an improvisation.

Sha bop sha bway bway

Zah doodle dwee dway dway

Bah dah bah dah bley bley

She be dah she be day

Sha doodle dlee sha doodle dlay

Bee doh blee bee doh bah

Sha va voo va dah day

Sha bah doo deh dley

Bee dle bee dle bley

Shoh doh day shoh doh day

Da bah da bah da doo

Spe dle dee doo spe dle dee dah

Spe lee dee bop dee bop

Zab doo dah zab doo day

Zah beh doo dlap

Sha blah blee sha bah blay

Zone zah doo zone zah zay

Shom boo bah shom boo bey

Doo doh doo dah doo doh doo dah

Splee dee doodle dow

Sue dooble dee dep sue dooble dee dow

Sple leh lee leap, sple leh lee lao

Bee de lee blue bee de lee blah

Fih fleh dih day fih fley dih dao

Bah dee din bah deed ah day
Bah deep dap bah dih dap
Deh ye deh ye dable day dah
Bah dee din dahya dahya don

TONGUE TWISTERS

A very fun way to practice the articulation of consonants is by saying tongue twisters. Notice which articulators are activated for each tongue twister. Have fun! Try to speak them faster and faster.

Six sick slick slim sycamore saplings.

A box of biscuits, a batch of mixed biscuits.

Peter Piper picked a peck of pickled peppers.
Did Peter Piper pick a peck of pickled peppers?
If Peter Piper picked a peck of pickled peppers,
where's the peck of pickled peppers Peter Piper picked?

Red lorry, yellow lorry, red lorry, yellow lorry.

Unique New York.

Betty Botter had some butter,
"But," she said, "this butter's bitter.
If I bake this bitter butter,
it would make my batter bitter.
But a bit of better butter,
that would make my batter better."
So she bought a bit of butter,
better than her bitter butter,
and she baked it in her batter,

and the batter was not bitter.
So 'twas better Betty Botter
bought a bit of better butter.

Six thick thistle sticks. Six thick thistles stick.

Toy boat. Toy boat. Toy boat.

One smart fellow, he felt smart.
Two smart fellows, they felt smart.
Three smart fellows, they all felt smart.

Mrs. Smith's Fish Sauce Shop.

Lesser leather never weathered wetter weather better.

Cheap ship trip.

Lovely lemon liniment.

Tim, the thin twin tinsmith.

Fat frogs flying past fast.

Flee from fog to fight flu fast!

Greek grapes.

Moose noshing much mush.

Six short slow shepherds.

Black bug's blood.

Crisp crusts crackle crunchily.

A tree toad loved a she-toad
who lived up in a tree.
He was a two-toed tree toad
but a three-toed toad was she.
The two-toed tree toad tried to win
the three-toed she-toad's heart,
for the two-toed tree toad loved the ground
that the three-toed tree toad trod.
But, the two-toed tree toad tried in vain.
He couldn't please her whim.
From her tree toad bower,
with her three-toed power,
the she-toad vetoed him.

Peggy Babcock.

Old oily Ollie oils old oily autos.

Nine nice night nurses nursing nicely.

Red leather, yellow leather.

The two-twenty-two train tore through the tunnel.

Twelve twins twirled twelve twigs.

Three gray geese in the green grass grazing.
Gray were the geese and green was the grass.

Many an anemone sees an enemy anemone.

If Stu chews shoes, should Stu choose the shoes he chews?

Give papa a cup of proper coffee in a copper coffee cup.

Plague-bearing prairie dogs.

Ed had edited it.

She sifted thistles through her thistle-sifter.

Good blood, bad blood.

DICTION TEXT

A really fun text to use to practice precise articulation skills is "The Major General's Song" from "The Pirates of Penzance." Speak the text below and try to go faster and faster, crisply articulating each consonant.

I am the very model of a modern Major General,
I've information vegetable, animal, and mineral,
I know the kings of England, and I quote the fights historical,
From Marathon to Waterloo, in order categorical;
I'm very well acquainted, too, with matters mathematical,
I understand equations, both the simple and quadratical,
About binomial theorem I'm teeming with a lot o' news,
With many cheerful facts about the square of the hypotenuse.
I'm very good at integral and differential calculus;
I know the scientific names of beings animalculous:

In short, in matters vegetable, animal, and mineral,
I am the very model of a modern Major General.
I know our mythic history, King Arthur's and Sir Caradoc's;
I answer hard acrostics, I've a pretty taste for paradox,
I quote in elegiacs all the crimes of Heliogabalus,
In conics I can floor peculiarities parabolous;
I can tell undoubted Raphaels from Gerard Dows and
Zoffanies,
I know the croaking chorus from the Frogs of Aristophanes!
Then I can hum a fugue of which I've heard the music's din afore,
And whistle all the airs from that infernal nonsense Pinafore.
Then I can write a washing bill in Babylonic cuneiform,
And tell you ev'ry detail of Caractacus's uniform:
In short, in matters vegetable, animal, and mineral,
I am the very model of a modern Major General.
In fact, when I know what is meant by "mamelon" and "ravelin,"
When I can tell at sight a Mauser rifle from a javelin,
When such affairs as sorties and surprises I'm more wary at,
And when I know precisely what is meant by "commissariat,"
When I have learnt what progress has been made in modern
gunnery,
When I know more of tactics than a novice in a nunnery,
In short, when I've a smattering of elemental strategy,
You'll say a better Major General has never sat a gee.
For my military knowledge, though I'm plucky and adventury,
Has only been brought down to the beginning of the century;
But still, in matters vegetable, animal, and mineral,
I am the very model of a modern Major General.

The ancient traditions of yoga teach that there are invisible energy channels within the body called nadis that course alongside and in the center of the spine. A wonderful result of voice work can be the opening of these channels.

Chapter Fourteen

SPEECH TIPS

YOUR AUTHENTIC VOICE

WHAT IS THE AUTHENTIC VOICE? I actually do not meet that many people, especially women, who speak using their authentic voice. The exploration of the primal voice is very helpful to uncover the authentic voice, the voice that comes from deep inside and has not been altered to sound more nice or sweet. Social customs begin impinging on our primal voice when we are very young. One of the favorite things for a toddler to do is play with his or her voice. Most of us are allowed, at a young age, to play with our voices. As we get older and become more aware of our environment, most of us will stop vocal play and start to alter our voice to fit social restraints. By the time we get to school, we are taught that a quiet child is a good child and girls should only talk sweetly. Instantly, our authentic voice is gone. Even so, we will experience our primal voice during intense crying or wailing and sometimes laughter, when our primal voice will unconsciously release. I have all of my students do some wailing and yelling exercises to open up the voice. This is not easy for many people. I actually have students who are incapable of yelling or wailing. Their throats clamp shut or there is so much tension in their throats and chests that they can only produce small, weak sounds. Today, to have the powerful voice required for the current vocal styles of singing, it is especially important to be able to yell. Actors must be able to yell. An actor cannot have vocal limitations. For day-to-day life, you must be able to produce a loud sound. You may need to call out for a taxi, call for a waiter in a crowded restaurant or speak in a noisy room. The ability to produce a loud sound may ensure safety. You may need to call out to alert a child of impending danger.

WAILING

Take a look at the exercises earlier in the book that show you how to vocalize pressing your hands against the wall, or putting your middle back against the wall. Press or lean into the wall and relax your throat so that it feels like a wide, round cylinder. Take a breath and let out a long wail on ahhhh. You can add a bit of the sound of a cry into the middle of the wail. Try to get the wail to come from deep inside your body, connected to the core. Add some emotion to the wail. What does this feel like? Try sliding up and down the scale while wailing.

LAUGHING

Right now, get a watch or clock with a second hand and see if you can laugh loudly for one straight minute. Notice how much energy it takes to laugh and where you feel the muscles activate in your body. Now try laughing for a minute again and experiment with different pitches and sounds. You could laugh on Hi Hi Ha Ha Ho Ho Wha Ha Hoo Hoo.

CRYING

Use your watch or clock with a second hand again and see if you can fake cry loudly for one straight minute. Notice how much energy it takes to make crying sounds. Where do you feel the muscles activate inside your body? Crying uses the ribs in an interesting way. Instead of opening the ribcage, as in breathing, crying squeezes the ribcage closed. The ribs squeeze inward when we cry. The actor can muscularly squeeze the ribcage inward to simulate the act of crying. Now try pretending to cry for a minute and experiment with different pitches and sounds.

MINDFUL BREATHING AND SPEAKING

Many forms of yoga and Buddhism speak of the benefits of mindful breathing. Being aware of your breathing brings you in the moment instantly, calms your nervous system and gives you an opportunity to reach self-realization. If we take our awareness one step deeper and are mindfully aware of our voice use, we will connect deeper to our truth and speak from that place. Mindful voice use will make us more aware of what we are saying and more in tune to the wonderful sensations of sound created through voice use.

VOCAL FRY AND WEAK VOICE USE

Very often, I get voice students who speak on the very lowest notes of their register in what we call a vocal fry. Vocal fry is a lazy vocal production that uses very little energy and produces a voice that sounds like a creaky door. Speaking in a devitalized voice is something that voice teachers do not like to see. Whispering or speaking with weak tone is more fatiguing for the voice than speaking louder, with full tone. One of the things we always tell voice students is not to whisper when they are sick. When people are sick with a sore throat, they will sometimes whisper instead of speaking with full tone. Voice therapists will immediately tell them to not whisper, because extended whispering can be hard on the vocal cords. When people whisper, they do not allow their vocal cords to completely close, resulting in a breathy sound. When whispering or using a breathy voice, instead of the vocal cords closing along their entire length, they close partially, leaving a chink at the bottom in which the sound of rushing air can escape. Regular voice use usually has complete closure along the full length of the vocal cords, preventing air-escape and noise during sounding. A creaky voice typically occurs when the vocal folds are tightly closed but weakly tensed, thus creating low airflow and slack vocal cords. Speaking with a breathy or creaky voice can fatigue your voice. To speak with pure tone usually requires the speaker to add energy, connect to the breath and speak a few notes higher than the bottom of his or her register.

A weak voice does not make a speaker sound calm or confident. If you want to make other people feel calm, a rich resonant voice is actually more useful. What actor, public announcer or TV newscaster has the voice that we are drawn to on TV? Who, in everyday life, attracts our attention purely by sound? Someone with a rich, full resonant tone will draw you toward them. The public also finds pure resonance much more soothing. Remember the voice of Martin Luther King. People who are in leadership positions most often possess rich resonant voices, not devitalized breathy, thin voices. Politicians, TV newscasters, radio hosts, corporate heads and actors usually have had voice training. With training, a beautiful rich voice is available to most public speakers.

By finding one's voice, one may also find one's own power. Most people find that when they discover that they have a rich, powerful voice within them, they feel a newly found sense of power and confidence.

There are exercises for speech therapy that use a specific type of vocal fry production. In this section, I am not referring to the vocal fry that a speech therapist or singing teacher might have you do. I don't use vocal fry exercises, but some teachers do for a specific vocal production problem.

> *Someone with a rich resonant voice will draw you toward them. People who are in leadership positions most often possess resonant voices.*

Mindful awareness of the link between our voice and our core forges a deep connection to our truth, from which speech can flow.

Chapter Fifteen

Be a More Expressive Speaker

EXPRESS YOURSELF

RATE OF SPEECH

Slowing down one's rate of speech can be one of the most difficult changes for some people to make. Many speakers are misunderstood simply because they talk too fast. If you talk too quickly, it can be difficult for other people to understand what you are saying. Speaking slower requires the speaker to lengthen vowel production, articulate consonants more clearly and connect the voice to the core of the body.

Speak the following passage out loud. If it takes you approximately 45 seconds, then you are speaking at an optimum rate. If it takes only 35 seconds, then you are speaking too fast. Try speaking the passage out loud again, while clearly enunciating every consonant. Do not forget the ending consonants. Did your rate of speech slow down?

Practice Passage

When the sunlight strikes raindrops in the air, they act as a prism and form a rainbow. The rainbow is a division of white light into many beautiful colors. These take the shape of a long round arch, with its path high above, and its two ends apparently beyond the horizon. There is, according to legend, a boiling pot of gold at one end. People look, but no one ever finds it. When a man looks for something beyond his reach, his friends say he is looking for the pot of gold at the end of the rainbow. Throughout the centuries, people have explained the rainbow in various ways. Some have accepted it as a miracle without physical explanation.

AVOID MONOTONE SPEAKING

It is important to vary the pitch in speech to avoid monotone speaking. A monotone speaker is someone who speaks on the same pitch at the same volume, continuously. Anyone who has ever gone to school has encountered the monotone speaker. A professor who speaks on just a few notes and does not change the volume at which he speaks can easily put a class to sleep. A monotone speaker can affect an audience in a manner similar to a hypnotist who is repeating something on the same pitch that your mind translates as, "You are now getting sleepy." There are all sorts of tricks that public speakers learn to make their speech more expressive and less monotone. Good public speakers learn to make specific changes in intonation that quickly make speech more expressive.

Intonation Changes

Here are some simple tools that you can utilize.

Allow the pitch of your voice to go up on words you want to stress. Notice how the word "viciously" stands out if you raise your vocal pitch on it.

The victim was "viciously" attacked.

Allow the pitch of your voice to move downward after important upward inflections. The second part of the sentence is not as exciting as the first part, so you want to lower your vocal pitch on it.

The bomb was about to go off in just under 20 seconds, 3 seconds faster than the last bomb he had to defuse.

Change the pitch of your voice between different transitions of thought. Otherwise, the distinction between each separate thought will not be understood.

I can't find my purse. By the way, my mother's coming to visit next week. Oh, you have to pick up the kids today.

Vary the pitch of your voice on items in a series so that the items do not blur together.

Many planets surround the sun: Mercury, Saturn, Mars and Neptune.

He was tired of listening to his mother-in-law, cooking for his mother-in-law, driving his mother-in-law and ignoring his mother-in-law.

Vary vocal pitch when explaining words or phrases. The pitch usually goes downward in the middle, explanatory section.

The lungs, two balloons of air in the chest, allow us to breathe fully.

Most speakers have a full, musical octave range of pitches available to sound on. That means there are twelve available notes for the speaker to use to make a speech exciting. Try the previous exercises again. Can you raise and lower your voice more as you make the pitch changes required?

TEACHERS ARE PROFESSIONAL VOICE USERS

Why does a teacher need to do voice work? Teachers are dependent on their voices for their livelihood. The role of a teacher is to communicate and educate. If a teacher can't talk, how can she communicate? If she can't communicate, then she can't educate. Teachers are, in fact, professional voice users even if they don't know it. They use their voices for more extended periods of time than everyday speakers. They often need to speak louder than conversational speech. Due to extended voice use and increased volume, teachers are one of the highest risk groups for voice injuries. Teachers make up a significant portion of an ear, nose and throat doctor's patient base. Usually, after an examination, the teacher is sent to a speech pathologist to learn how to use their voice correctly. Some teachers adapt to extended voice work and figure out how to find the right support muscles for the voice . . . lucky them! However, most teachers need some instruction on how to power the voice from the diaphragm and abdominal muscles. Without some training, most teachers will continue trying to power the voice from the throat, causing strain and possible vocal injury. Because the vocal cords are muscles, you can strain, sprain, hemorrhage and irritate them.

Singers, actors and business professionals train for performance just like athletes. They learn to transform nervous energy into start-up energy.

Part Five

PERFORMANCE

SKILLS

According to psychological surveys, public speaking is the number one fear, so singing is off the charts.

Chapter Sixteen

IN PERFORMANCE

FIGHT OR FLIGHT

The Autonomic Nervous System Response and Singing in Public

PERFORMING IS NOT A NATURAL exercise and public singing can be extremely uncomfortable. For many, the performing arts, especially singing, can create the most extreme fear and intense reaction of the autonomic nervous system. Many an experienced actor has been reduced to a trembling novice at the mere thought of a singing performance. The first part, in the process of learning to perform, is to understand the behavior of your own autonomic nervous system, the nervous system that is unconscious. Start by observing how it manifests in your body. When your body is taken out of its comfort zone and put into a scary scenario, like singing in front of an audience, many extreme physical and mental reactions may occur. To be able to control these autonomic reactions and sing, the performer has to first analyze his or her body's specific autonomic responses. Each person will have very specific autonomic reflexes that are unique to him or her. If you don't know what your symptoms are, you can become swept away in a general, overall panic. It is important to begin learning how to mentally disconnect from the symptoms you experience, while watching the body's autonomic nervous system in full swing.

Some of the symptoms experienced can be:

Body Symptoms

A racing heart
Heat all over the body
Tremors, especially in the knees and legs if you are standing
Muscle clenching
Sweaty palms
Hand clenching
Breath holding
Tightness in the throat
Dry mouth
Frequent urination
Nausea

Mental Symptoms

Brain fog
Memory loss
A sense of panic
A mental state of extreme danger
Extreme fear
Anger or irritability
Extreme sense of embarrassment
The urge to flee out the door
Afterwards, a desire to judge oneself negatively

You must kill your inner critic to succeed. Beware of criticism from family and friends who mean well. Surround yourself with positive people who support you in your artistic ventures.

*Your resistance is your negativity; we all have it.
If you are not aware of your negativity, it will be
difficult for you to reach your dream.*

Chapter Seventeen

RESISTANCE

DON'T GIVE IN!

A VERY INTERESTING ASPECT OF voice work is that, when dealing with expanding one's voice, one also often encounters resistance. Resistance is your negativity. We all have it and we will all encounter it when we try to expand and grow. Growth is not always comfortable. In voice work, many people, at first, are uncomfortable with risking self expression, especially in front of other people. Learning voice technique helps build confidence. Once you have learned how your voice works and have technique, you have only to step into your brilliance. But, many people will encounter resistance when attempting to be brilliant. "Who do you think you are?" your snake of negativity might hiss in your ear. Milton Katselas, the famous acting teacher, called our negativity our snake, and he said that you must kill your snake to succeed. He said that you must pick up the warrior's sword and slice the snake into tiny bits.

Write down all your negative thoughts regarding your voice or any dream that you have. If you are a singer or actor, write down every negative thought you have about singing or acting and pursuing a career in singing or acting. Everything on this list is your resistance and an excuse to avoid your brilliance. Become aware of comments friends and family make. Friends and family sometimes unconsciously don't want you to be successful. They have their own inner snakes hissing in their ears, and many of them have given up on their dreams. Most families in America belong to the middle class and middle-class values are all about playing it safe and conformity. If you tell your middle-class family that you are dropping out of law school to become a singer or actor, they will probably be unhappy. Middle-class values are about getting a secure job and playing it safe. Artistry is about risking and pushing boundaries.

Resistance and Practicing

One of the main ways resistance shows up for many people is by interfering with their practice schedule. Set aside 20 minutes a day to practice. If you don't practice, write down all of the excuses of resistance that kept you from practicing. What did you make more important than your dream? What did you make more important than you?

Once you look at your list, start to become aware of your negativity and see how it restricts you. If you are not aware of your negativity, it will interfere with your ability to succeed at any dream you have. It will tell you that you are too young, too old, too fat, too skinny, not pretty enough, too pretty, not talented enough, too talented, too tired, and that you don't have enough money or time to follow your dream.

Chapter Eighteen

Power Performance Tools

START IT UP!

ACCORDING TO PSYCHOLOGICAL STUDIES, PUBLIC speaking is the number one fear that most people have, so singing is off the charts. Death is the number two fear, so most people would rather die than speak or sing in public. Here are some exercises that can help you deal with performance anxiety and have a winning performance.

START-UP ENERGY

Singers, actors and business professionals train for performances just like athletes. Still, many people always have activation of their autonomic nervous system before singing or speaking in public. Many athletes also have active autonomic reactions before competitions and must learn to transform their autonomic energy into what they call "start-up energy." Studies have found that singers and actors who have start-up energy before performing often perform better than singers or actors who feel mellow and laid-back. The same has been found for athletes and, since vocal performing is similar to athletic performing, many professional singers and actors use the same behavior modification tools and power performance exercises as athletes.

SYMPTOMS EXERCISE

Get up and sing in front of a class or group. Pay attention only to the physical and mental autonomic reactions that are happening in your body. Don't be concerned with singing well, remembering lyrics or entertaining anyone. Become a watcher of how your body reacts to performing; awareness is the first step. After singing, write down all the physical sensations you experienced in your body and all the mental symptoms you experienced in your mind. Your singing technique may go out the window when you first start performing. Much of the training for singing is training the body to function with muscle memory during a performance. A well-trained singer will be able to perform no matter what is going on in his or her mind or autonomic nervous system. The body will know what to do to produce a beautiful sound even if the singer is completely freaked out.

FALSE INFORMATION EXERCISE

When you are about to sing or speak in public, your fight or flight mechanism may become very active and it may send your mind signals of danger. FEAR is an acronym for "false evidence appearing real." The fight or flight mechanism may give you false evidence that appears very real at the moment. But it is lying to you. You will not die if you speak or sing in public. After you finish singing, notice that you are still alive and nothing truly terrible has happened to you. Though your autonomic nervous system warned you that you were in extreme danger, this was not true. Look at your list of physical and mental symptoms and cross off everything that was false information.

RELAXATION EXERCISES

Any sort of muscle relaxation exercise is beneficial to the singer. My favorite is the clench and release. Go through each part of your body, starting at your feet, and clench the muscles for a count of three, and then release. On the count of one, squeeze the muscle a little bit, on two, a little more and on three, squeeze the muscle as hard as you can, without hurting yourself. This is the best way to relax muscles. By squeezing the muscle, it can completely let go on the release.

FEET SPINE PREPARATION EXERCISE

Don't forget to do the feet spine preparation exercise that is in the beginning section of this book. This is a quick but very effective preparation for singing, acting or public speaking. It is also great for people with performance anxiety, as it gives the mind something to do in those seconds before singing, when one can become anxious.

BREATHING EXERCISES

Breathing is one of the best ways to find your center and calm the nervous system. Find your feet with your mind and then find your spine. Put your hands on the lower part of your ribcage. Take a slow breath inhaling on a count of five, allowing the ribcage to float open on the sides and lift gently up in the front. Keep the lower abdominal muscles free and relaxed. Suspend (don't inhale or exhale) for a count of five, without closing the glottis (the opening between the vocal cords), and exhale on a count of five. Gradually increase your count all the way to 10.

Inhale	Suspend	Exhale
12345--------------------12345------------------12345		
123456-------------------123456------------------123456		
1234567-----------------1234567-----------------1234567		

Add counting. Do the exercise again, and when you are at the suspend stage of the exercise, count out loud, first to five, and then consecutively up to 10.

SAVE IT FOR LATER BAG

Often, when a singer gets ready to perform, insecurities or negative thoughts that have been sitting in the unconscious part of the mind can surface. Acknowledge these thoughts and tell them that you can't think of them right now. Then put them in a mental "save it for later" bag and address them after the performance.

VISUALIZE A WIN

Picture yourself performing. Put all the details in the visualization. What does the room look like, what does the audience look like, what are you wearing? Sing your song and make it be the best singing you have ever done. You are the world's greatest singer! Imagine the audience going wild with appreciation.

AFFIRMATIONS

Make up your own positive affirmations and then use them. You must repeat your affirmations over and over. If a negative thought comes in, push it out and replace it with a positive thought. You can affirm things like, "I am the world's greatest singer."

WHAT COULD GO WRONG LIST

Some people are natural worriers. Many students will ask me before a performance, "What will I do if I trip, what will I do if I forget my words, what if, what if, what if.....??!!" If you know that you are one of these people, then the following exercise is very good for you, especially if you are someone who starts to worry the week before a performance. Take out a sheet of paper and write on the left side, "What if this goes wrong?" On the right side, write down all the possible solutions. Create a solution for every possible thing that could go wrong. If you have a solution for every possible mishap, then you are prepared for anything.

CELEBRATION

After every performance, no matter how small, you must celebrate. Speaking in public is the number one fear for most people, and singing is off the charts; so if you get up and speak or sing in public, celebrate afterwards. If you jumped out of an airplane, you would definitely celebrate afterwards. Performing is a huge leap and, even though your life was not truly threatened, you still need to celebrate. Getting up and letting the world hear your voice is a huge achievement. Throw your critic out the window and celebrate more.

PRACTICE

Eventually, you will be able to implement all of the techniques of good voice production under the pressures of performing. In time, even a sense of pleasure and satisfaction can be derived from performing. Being comfortable takes practice, so practice everywhere that you can.

SINGING IN PUBLIC AND FIREWALKING

The experience of performing is very similar to firewalking. In the early eighties, I walked on hot burning coals with Tony Robbins, the motivational speaker, when he first began teaching seminars. The 20 seminar participants and I watched Tony put coals on the ground, set them on fire and let them cook to a hot temperature. We then chanted cool moss, over and over, and walked across the hot burning coals barefoot, without any damage to our feet. Before I walked across the coals, my brain was freaking out. I was convinced that I was going to injure myself. But I kept chanting cool moss, and when I got to the other side, I looked at my bare feet and they were fine. My brain became so confused. It had warned me repeatedly about the danger of fire, but I was not injured. So, my brain had not really told me the truth. Immediately, I had the extreme awareness of the separation of my brain and my real soul-self. "Well, if you are not going to listen to me," said my brain, "then I am going to be quiet." What remained was a wonderful state of quiet and peace. I had a sense of being more present and "in the moment" than I had ever experienced before. I also had a feeling of joyful exhilaration. I imagine skydiving has a similar effect. Like firewalking, performing is a wonderful opportunity to take us out of our comfort zones and overcome our fears. I have had students who were skydivers tell me that singing in public was scarier than skydiving. So, allow yourself to be scared and perform in spite of your fear; a sense of exhilaration may be waiting on the other side.

For many, the performing arts, especially singing, can create an intense reaction of the autonomic nervous system's fight or flight response.

Find an uplifting or motivational song and make it your theme song. Sing it each day and keep the blues away.

Chapter Nineteen

TIPS FOR SONG CHOICE

SING A SONG YOU LIKE

PICK A SONG THAT YOU like to sing. If the song speaks to you in some way, or has a message that you want to convey, you will give a better performance. Voice teachers will pick repertoire for students to sing in order to work on specific techniques. However, if you dislike a song, ask your teacher if he or she has another song in the same realm that you could sing. Your teacher won't know if you hate a song unless you speak up. If you hate the song you are given, you won't practice it, so you need to ask for a song you like. Do be open-minded to trying different styles. A teacher will often give a student a particular style of song in an attempt to bring out certain attributes in the voice, which, in turn, will strengthen and support the style of music that the student is interested in.

SHOW YOUR VOICE

Sing a song that shows your voice. Some songwriters are not singers and write songs that don't bring out the beauty of the voice. In contrast, there are some songs that feel good to the voice immediately; the voice just flows out easily and feels nurtured by the song.

HOW TO PICK A SONG KEY

When you are picking out a song to sing, you must examine the range of the song. The range is the distance between the lowest note and the highest note. Always try to pick a song key where you can comfortably sing all the notes. You always want to start singing a song somewhere around your natural speaking pitch, and then from there, extend your vocal range up and down the scale. One of the ways to find your range is to start singing a song a cappella on the first note that easily comes to you. We will often gravitate to a natural key if we don't think too much about it. Then check to see if you can reach the highest note and the lowest note. If not, adjust the key up or down until all the notes are comfortable. Sometimes a song will require too wide a range for your voice. If so, put that song on the back burner and work on range extension exercises for a while. Then you can revisit the song and see whether or not you are able to hit the notes. If not, you may need to take a realistic look at your voice and decide whether or not the song is too difficult for you.

In performance, always sing songs that will show off the assets of your voice. We always want to hide any shortcomings in our voice. I call it, "hiding the seams of your garment." If you made a shirt, you wouldn't want any loose threads or sloppy seams to be seen on the outside, so you wouldn't, as the aphorism goes, "wear them on your sleeve." The audience who attends your performance is there to be entertained. They don't care if you have a three-octave range or if you can hit the highest or lowest notes that exist. More often, they don't know that much about music and will not notice many small things that seem obvious to the performer. The audience is always more interested in the overall performance. For example, I had a student that had to sing the song "All That Jazz" for a vocal contest. She was also a dancer, so she choreographed the number. Although we put the song in a comfortable key, she couldn't consistently hit the highest, last note of the song. Instead of obsessing over that one note, she dropped into splits on the last note, lifted her hat to the judges and speak-sang it. Do you think the judges noticed? Not at all, she won second place.

Songwriters, write a song that is in your comfortable vocal range. I often hear songwriters who write songs in keys that are way too high for them to sing. If you are creating a song, create it to fit your range and show off the positive features of your voice. Find where the most brilliant, powerful notes (the notes we call the money notes) in your voice are and write the climax of the song on these notes. You are the creator as a songwriter. Create a world in which you will soar.

BREATHING IN A SONG

Once a song has been picked, the first thing the singer must do is to go through the song and mark, using a big comma or check mark, the places to take a breath. The singer should learn where to breathe in a song at the same time he or she is learning the words and the music. Then, the places for breathing will become automatic and, when the singer performs, there will be no awkward breaths taken between words or on illogical beats. Also, when a performer is nervous, the first thing that the performer forgets to do is to breathe. If the breaths are imprinted in the mind of the performer as strongly as the words and music, there is less chance of a dropped breath.

One of the ways to decide where to breathe is to look at the punctuation in the text. The punctuation shows you where the composer has broken up the phrases and where he or she wants you to breathe. A period or comma is an obvious break in the phrase and the first place that you will mark for breathing on your sheet music. Sometimes a phrase is too long and needs to be divided into parts. To find a logical place to break up the phrase, speak the phrase and see where you might make a pause in natural speech. Find a place where, if you breathed, the pause would not distort the meaning of the phrase or sound awkward. Sometimes there may be more than one place where you can break up the phrase. In this situation, you get to make an artistic choice. For example, "The rain in Spain stays mainly on the plain." You could break up the phrase at, "The rain in Spain (breath) stays mainly on the plain." Or you could say, "The rain in Spain stays mainly (breath) on the plain." Either choice is viable. All that matters is that the phrase makes sense.

Sometimes songs have rests between phrases. A rest in the music is always a logical choice for a place to take a breath. The composer doesn't want you to sing during a rest, hence the placement of the rest.

Sometimes a singer will forget to take a breath. That is why it is important to be able to do the catch breath. Remember, a singer is a song communicator, so make sure that your phrasing best communicates the meaning of the phrase.

> *Being a perfectionist can be death for an artist.*
> *Perfectionism puts the artist in a box, and the more*
> *the artist tries to be perfect, the smaller and smaller*
> *the box gets, until the artist cannot move.*

Chapter Twenty

FINAL THOUGHTS

EXPRESSIONISM, NOT PERFECTIONISM

BEING A PERFECTIONIST CAN BE death for an artist. Perfectionism puts the artist in a box, and the more the artist tries to be perfect, the smaller and smaller the box gets, until the artist cannot move. I have seen many people give up on their artistic dream because they could not be perfect. One must learn to create for the joy of creating and expressing. Many fantastic performers don't have the best voices, but they have a desire to express themselves and something to say. Bob Dylan and Leonard Cohen are two examples of amazing artists who were not gifted with perfect voices. Their lack of vocal finesse did not affect their careers one bit. There is nothing wrong with trying to be the best you can be, but make your goal expressionism, not perfectionism. If you focus on expressing yourself as an artist, you will be fulfilled. If you focus your attention on being perfect, you will never be satisfied, as that day will never come. We are human, so there will always be moments of imperfection.

DO ART BECAUSE YOU LOVE IT

You must enjoy the process of making your art and not be as concerned with the end result. If you love what you are doing, you will want to do it often, and since you are doing it often, you will become good at it. Art will only enrich your life; it is never time wasted. I sometimes meet people who want to be singers and actors but they never sing or act. They are in love with the idea of being something but not the art itself. Rarely will people like this succeed.

HAVE A THEME SONG

Have you noticed how, when you sing, you automatically feel happy? It is very hard to be in a bad mood when you sing. Therefore, I think everyone should have a theme song.

Pick a song that is inspirational to you, a song that speaks to you in some way, and memorize it. Start to use your song anytime you are stressed or need an emotional lift. Driving is a great time to practice your song, especially on your way to work. Singing is a great way to wake up in the morning and go to bed at night. No one has to hear you or know your theme song. It is your special song, just for you. You can also have a family theme song. When I was in high school, every morning my brother and I would turn on the song "Good Morning" by the Beatles and sing and dance to it. I was in a great mood the rest of the day. A family who sings together is a happy family. Abraham Lincoln said, "We are only as happy as we decide to be." Having singing in your life will only bring you joy.

Bibliography

Appelman, D. Ralph. *The Science of Vocal Pedagogy*. Bloomington, IN: Indiana University Press, 1986.

Bander, Ratziel. *The Miracle of Hsin Tao*. Los Angeles: Hsin Tao Institute, 2005.

Brown, William Earl. *Vocal Wisdom: Maxims of Giovanni Battista Lamperti*. Whitefish, MT: Kessinger Publishing LLC, 2008.

Caccini, Guilio. *Nuove Musiche*. 2nd ed. Ed. Wiley K. Hitchcock. Middleton, WI: A-R Editions, 1979.

Caruso, Enrique, and Luisa Tetrazzini. *Caruso and Tetrazzini on the Art of Singing*. New York: Dover Publications Inc., 1975.

Christy, Van A. *Foundations in Singing*. Dubuque, IA: Wm C. Brown Company Publishers, 1979.

Coffin, Bernard. *Historical Vocal Pedagogy Classics*. Metuchen, NJ: Scarecrow Press, 1989.

Emmons, Shirley, and Alma Thomas. *Power Performance for Singers*. New York: Oxford University Press, 1998.

Fields, Victor Alexander. *Training the Singing Voice: An Analysis of the Working Concepts Contained in Recent Contributions to Vocal Pedagogy*. New York: Kings Crown Press, 1947.

Fitzmaurice, Catherine. "Breathing is Meaning." *The Vocal Vision*. Ed. Marian Hampton. New York: Applause Books, 1997. 247-252.

Frisell, Anthony. *The Tenor Voice*. Boston, MA: Brandon Publishing Co, 2003.

Garcia, Manual. *A Complete Treatise on the Art of Singing, Part I*. 1847 and 1972 Editions. Ed. and Trans. Donald V. Paschke. New York: De Capo Press, 1975.

————. *Hints on Singing*. New York: Joseph Patelson Music House LTD., 1982.

Gray, Henry. *Anatomy of the Human Body*. Philadelphia, PA: Lea & Febiger, 1918. http://www.bartleby.com/107.

Heirich, Jane Ruby. *Voice and the Alexander Technique*. Berkeley, CA: Mornum Time Press, 2005.

Lamperti, Francesco. *The Art of Singing*. Trans. J.C. Griffith. Boca Raton, FL: Kalmus Classic Editions, 1928.

Lamperti, Giovanni Battista. *The Techniques of Bel Canto*. New York: G. Schirmer, 1905.

Leanderson, R., J. Sundberg, and C. Von Euler. "Breathing Muscle Activity and Subglottal Pressure Dynamics in Singing and Speech." *KTH Dept. for Speech, Music and Hearing Quarterly Progress and Status Report Journal* 27. 4 (1986): 057-064.

Life, David. "To Infinity and Beyond," *Yoga Journal Online*, El Segundo, CA: Active Interest Media, 2009. http://www.yogajournal.com.

Linklater, Kristin. *Freeing the Natural Voice*. New York: Drama Book Publishers, 1976.

Mancini, Giambattista. *Practical Reflections on Figured Singing*. Trans. Pietro Buzzi. Boston, MA: Gorham Press, 1912.

Melton, Joan, and Kenneth Tom. *One Voice: Integrating Singing Technique and Theatre Voice Training*. Portsmouth, NH: Heinemann Drama, 2003.

Mercier, Patricia. *The Chakra Bible*. London: Sterling Publishing, 2007.

Miller, Richard. *On the Art of Singing.* New York: Oxford University Press, 1996.

―――. *National Schools of Singing.* Lanham, MD: Scarecrow Press, 1997.

―――. *Solutions for Singers.* New York: Oxford University Press, 2004.

―――. *The Structure of Singing.* New York: Schirmer Books, Macmillan, Inc., 1986.

Monahan, Brett Jeffrey. *The Art of Singing: a Compendium of Thoughts Published Between 1777 and 1927.* Metuchen, NJ: Scarecrow Press, 1978.

―――. *The Singer's Companion, a Guide to Improving Your Voice and Performance.* Pompton Plains, New Jersey: Limelight Editions, 2006.

Rodenburg, Patsy. *The Actor Speaks.* New York: Palgrave, Macmillan, 2002.

Shakespeare, William. *The Art of Singing.* Boston, MA: Oliver Ditson Company, 1910.

―――. *Plain Words on Singing.* London, England: Putnum Sons, 1924.

Skinner, Edith. *Speak With Distinction.* New York: Applause, 1990.

Stark, James. *Bel Canto, A History of Vocal Pedagogy.* Toronto, Canada: University of Toronto Press, 2003.

Swami Vivekananda. *The Yoga Sutras of Pantanjali.* London: Watson Publishing, 2007.

Titze, Ingo. *Principles of Voice Production.* Englewood Cliffs, New Jersey: Prentice-Hall, 1994.

Tosi, Pier Francesco. *Observations on the Florid Song.* London: William Reeves, 1723.

Turner, Clifford J. *Voice and Speech in the Theatre.* 5th ed. New York: Theatre Arts Books/Routledge, 2000.

Urla, Jonathan. "Every Breath You Take." *Pilates Style* 5. 1 Jan./Feb. (2008): 1-4.

Vennard, William. *Singing: The Mechanism and the Technic,* rev. ed. New York: Carl Fischer, 1967.

White, Ernest G. *Sinus Tone Production.* London: J.M. Dent & Sons Ltd., 1938.

Zemlin, Willard R. *Speech and Hearing Science, Anatomy and Physiology.* Needham Heights, MA: Allen and Bacon Press, 1998.

Index

Printed in Great Britain
by Amazon